UNIX System

Price Performance Guide

Winter/Spring 1994

AIM TECHNOLOGY

UNIX System Price Performance Guide

Subscription Service, Back Issues, Change of Address

The UNIX System Price Performance Guide is published quarterly by AIM Technology. Single copy price is $9.95, plus $3.50 shipping in the U.S. and Canada or $8.00 for international shipping. Subscriptions are $29.95, plus $15.00 shipping in the U.S. and Canada or $30.00 for international shipping. Send address changes and requests for subscriptions and back issues to: Subscription Director, AIM Technology, 4699 Old Ironsides Drive, Suite 150, Santa Clara, CA, 95054, or call AIM at (800) 848-8649 (in California, (408) 748-8649).

Permissions and Reprints

Material in this publication may not be reproduced in whole or in part without written permission from AIM Technology. To include any portion of this document in other publications, please contact the editor. For information on reprints, contact the Subscription Director.

How to Obtain Additional Information

Information in the Price Performance Guide is condensed. For additional background and technical details on a system, consult AIM Technology. If you are interested in a system that is not listed in this publication, please contact AIM and we will pass your request on to the manufacturer.

Letters to the Editor

Please send your comments, suggestions, or complaints to Editor, Price Performance Guide, c/o AIM Technology at the address noted below.

AIM Technology • 4699 Old Ironsides Drive, Suite 150 • Santa Clara, CA 95054 U.S.A.
Phone: (408) 748-8649 • Outside CA: (800) 848-UNIX • FAX: (408) 748-0161
email benchinfo@aim.com

Winter/Spring 1994 Edition

ISBN 1-881351-08-4
Printed in U.S.A.

Printed on recycled paper.

CONTENTS

ABOUT

AIM TECHNOLOGY

AIM Technology, established in 1981, is an independent organization that specializes in UNIX performance tools and services. AIM's goal is to provide consumers reliable information for UNIX system purchases.

All AIM ratings and reports in this publication are independently certified by AIM Technology. AIM Technology is not obligated to any outside commercial interest.

AIM products are used worldwide by virtually every computer manufacturer and are considered standards at hundreds of Fortune 1000 companies and international government agencies.

AIM Technology's Performance Measurement tools and services include:

Performance Tools

AIM Workstation Benchmark Suite VI

AIM Multiuser Benchmark Suite VII

AIM Independent Resource Benchmark - Suite IX

ANALYZE

AIM Subsystem Benchmark Suite II

AIM System Benchmark Suite III

AIM Utilities Benchmark Milestone

AIM X Windows Benchmark Suite X

Performance Services

Certified Workstation Report & Certification Services

Certified Multiuser Report & Certification Services

AIM Performance Report Certification Services

AIM Performance Report Series and Subscriptions

HOW TO USE THIS GUIDE

Our Mission

The goal of this guide is to present you, our readers, with system performance information that will help you make intelligent computer purchases quickly. To that end, this guide compares the performance of similar systems (Price/Performance Guides), presents new certified performance reports, and summarizes system price, configuration, and performance data (Buyer's Guide). This article describes how we compile this information and how to use this guide as you plan your computer purchases.

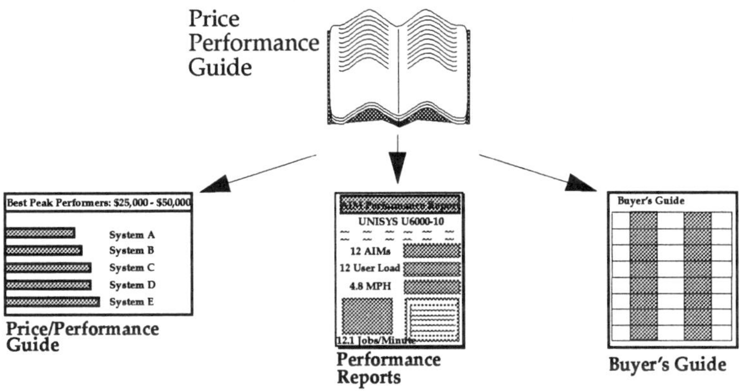

Testing Systems and Certifying Results

AIM has developed four system performance certification services. Each service is tailored for systems that perform specific types of tasks in specific environments:

AIM Performance Certification Service

AIM Workstation Certification Service

AIM Multiuser Certification Service

AIM X Windows Certification Service

Manufacturers use our services to test and certify system performance and publish the related AIM performance report (**AIM Performance Reports, AIM Certified Workstation Report, AIM Certified Multiuser Report**, and **AIM X Windows Performance Report**). When we publish a performance report, we store the system's price, configuration, and performance ratings in our database.

Comparing Performance Results

We use the information in our database to present and compare performance results in four sections: System Performance, Workstation Performance, Multiuser Performance, and X Windows Performance.

Each of these sections includes performance data in one or more of the following formats: Price/Performance Guides, performance reports, and a Buyer's Guide.

All three formats appear in the System Performance section of this guide. Performance reports also appear in the Workstation, Multiuser, and X Windows Performance sections.

Performance Section	Contents
System	Price/Performance Guides Reports Buyer's Guide
Workstation	Reports
Multiuser	Reports
X Windows	Reports

The following paragraphs describe each of these formats.

Price/Performance Guides

As we prepare each new edition of this quarterly guide, we compare the performance of similarly priced systems tested in the last year and develop a series of graphs (Price/Performance Guides) that compare how systems performed in the following areas:

Price versus Peak Performance - Identifies systems that reach their peak performance for the least cost.

Price versus Sustained Performance - Identifies systems that reach their maximum capacity for the least cost.

Peak Performance - Identifies the systems that are exceptionally powerful with one or more users who are occasionally very demanding.

Sustained Performance - Identifies systems that maintain high performance under heavy system loads.

In addition, we compare the peak and sustained performance of single-CPU RISC machines and single CPU machines based on Intel architecture. The graphs and the ratings used to develop them are described in the introduction to the System Performance section of this guide.

Certified Reports

Each edition of this guide includes the front page of all performance reports published since the last edition.

Buyer's Guide

The Buyer's Guide, a listing of all systems tested in the last year, includes each system's price, configuration, and performance ratings.

Using the Guide

Identify Performance Needs

To use this guide effectively you must know what type of performance is most critical in your environment: peak or sustained.

As mentioned earlier, Peak Performance identifies the systems that are exceptionally powerful with one or more users who are occasionally very demanding. If the system that you plan to purchase will experience this type of usage, you can purchase a more cost effective solution.

Sustained performance identifies systems that maintain high performance under heavy system loads. If the system that you plan to purchase will operate in this type of environment, you may require a higher capacity configuration. For workstations, sustained performance is a function of the amount of multitasking and application mixes in the environment. For multiuser systems, sustained performance is a function of the number of users that the system must support.

Select System

Now that you have identified the type of performance that you are looking for, select one of your systems to compare with other systems listed in this guide. Select a system that you are familiar with in terms of configuration and performance. Locate the system in this guide, and note the system's ratings. (If your system is not included in this guide, contact AIM about conducting a baseline test on your system.)

Compare Performance Ratings

Compare the system's performance ratings with the ratings of similarly priced systems. If your system is not meeting your performance requirements, look for systems with higher ratings.

When you locate a system or systems that will meet your performance requirements, request complete four-page certified reports from the manufacturer or AIM at (800) 848-8649.

ABOUT THIS ISSUE

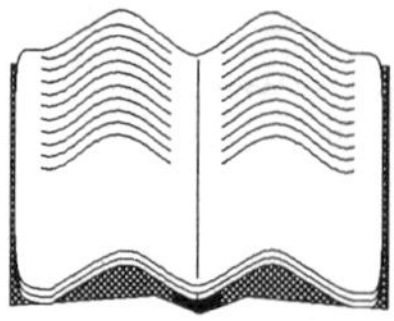

The Winter/Spring 1994 Edition

We've changed the name of this edition from "Winter" to "Winter/Spring." Our next issue, published in April, will be our Summer issue. If you have an annual subscription, you will still receive four editions of the guide.

NEW!!!

If you are familiar with AIM and the UNIX System Price Performance Guide, you will notice that this edition is different. AIM has recently introduced three new benchmarks and two new certification reports and services:

NEW Benchmarks

AIM Workstation Benchmark - Suite VI

AIM Multiuser Benchmark - Suite VII

AIM Independent Resource Benchmark - Suite IX

NEW Certified Reports

Certified Workstation Report

Certified Multiuser Report

NEW Certification Services

AIM Workstation Certification Service

AIM Multiuser Certification Service

These new benchmarks, reports, and services are described in this guide. As certified reports for workstation and multiuser systems are published, performance results will be presented in the same formats used for our flagship certification reports, the AIM Performance Reports.

To help make the new guide easier to use, we have added tabs that identify and separate each section.

Subscription Information

AIM's UNIX System Price Performance Guide is the most complete source of UNIX system performance information. Manufacturers, procurement specialists, and end-users find this guide to be an essential resource.

Make sure that you get all the latest performance information on UNIX systems. Order your subscription now. You'll receive four quarterly issues full of timely information for just $29.95. This annual subscription rate represents more than a 25% discount over the single copy price.

To order your subscription, call AIM Technology at (800) 848-8649 (outside California) or (408) 748-8649.

Improving File Performance

Making Your Current Systems Faster and Better

Feature

At the top of each AIM Performance Report is a section which details the system's configuration at test time. This information is presented to help you make an informed decision concerning a system's capabilities. A cursory glance through the pages of this guide should make one fact very clear: *system throughput is dependent on both CPU power and system configuration.* It is easy to artificially constrain a system by reducing its memory or I/O so that the CPU cannot stay busy. Alternately, by adding I/O and/or memory, a mundane configuration can become a "star."

System configurations are not cast in granite. In fact, the average system undergoes at least two major upgrades throughout its life. (In some government installations this number is 4 or 5.) These upgrades usually involve adding memory and/or I/O capacity. One of the major reasons for upgrading systems is that companies have found the need to add users or applications while at the same time improving overall system performance. Important new third party products become available as upgrade alternatives that can have a major impact on system performance.

Third party or "after market" products are playing an important role in more and more end-user environments. As a result, AIM has added a new section to this guide called "Special Interest" which will directly address this area of request. In this new section, we will publish pairs of results (before and after), to demonstrate the performance implications of upgrading a system with a specific product or products. Using this information, end-users can quickly narrow their searches for potential upgrade solutions and more efficiently address a range of solutions.

In this inaugural edition of the "Special Interest" section, AIM is pleased to point to the CASD products produced by Zitel Corporation of Fremont, Calif. CASD stands for "Cached Actuator Storage Device" and represents a class of "super disk" that is becoming available. CASD consists of a high performance disk along with up to 256 megabytes of battery-backed up RAM which acts as a reliable disk cache for both reads and writes. Special CASD-resident firmware keeps track of which disk locations are most probably going to be accessed in the near future and keeps them in memory. The batteries guarantee that in the case of a power failure, all data ultimately goes to disk — no data is lost.

CASD fits in the special interest category for several reasons: (1) it is not offered by system vendors, (2) it is a standard SCSI device which can be installed in the field and requires little or no specialized installation knowledge, and (3) it provides a high-performance solution to a common problem — disk bottlenecks.

While AIM is not recommending or endorsing CASD, systems with severe I/O bottlenecks may be helped by the use of CASD or similar products. Future additions of the special interest section will contain other performance-enhancing products including memory, controllers, RAM-disks, disk arrays, CPU-upgrades and a host of other ways to enhance performance. As always, when considering the addition of any system upgrade product, it is important to make sure that the performance of the component will be worthwhile on your configuration for your application environment. To this end, always ask for AIM Certified results for the appropriate workload mix, and system configuration, both before and after any upgrade.

You may find the performance improvements in the reports shown on pages 11 and 12 to be of interest. These were taken from Certified AIM results of the AIM Multiuser Benchmark - Suite VII using the "file server mix." AIM's enhanced load mix modeling allows simulation of the system's application environment. The results show substantial performance improvements in an I/O intensive environment.

Other performance comparisons appear in the Special Interests section of this guide. See the "After Market Spotlight: Zitel CASD Disk Add-on" table on page 133.

Certified Multiuser Report

AIM Technology

A UNIX Performance Summary Based on the AIM Multiuser Benchmark and the AIM Independent Resource Benchmark (Release 1.0)
File Server Mix

SUN SPARCserver 670

Price	*CPU Type*	*Clock Rate*	*1st Level Cache*	*2nd Level Cache*	*RAM*
N/A	SPARC	40 MHz	None	1 MB	64 MB

Disks	*Disk Controllers*	*I/O Buffers*	*O/S*	*File System*	*Compiler*
1.0 GB, 10.5ms	SCSI-II	Dynamic	Solaris 2.2	UFS	GNU C

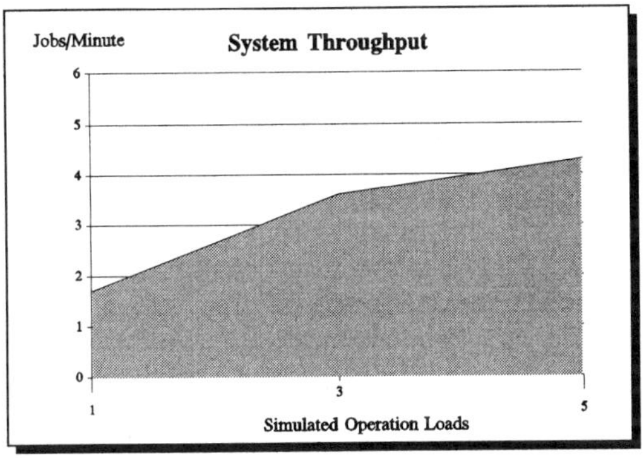

Peak Performance
4.3 AIM File Server Jobs/Minute

The **Peak Performance** reflects the system throughput at the point at which the system is able to process the most jobs per minute.

Sustained Performance
3.0 AIM File Server Loads

The **Sustained performance** indicates the multitasking operation load where the system's performance could become unacceptable, i.e. less than 1 job/minute/AIM File Server load.

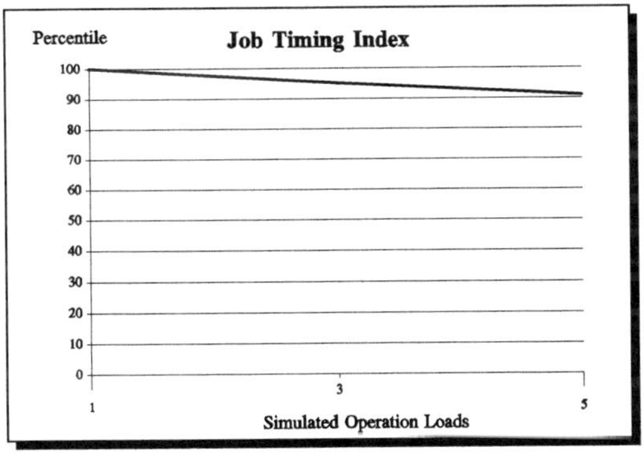

Job Timing Index
91 Percentile

The **Job Timing Index** is a measure of difference in completion times for concurrent jobs. It reveals the ability of a system to run processes simultaneously.

Certified By:

AIM Technology

Date: Dec 28, 1993
S/N# 0011

Certified Multiuser Report

AIM Technology

A UNIX Performance Summary Based on the AIM Multiuser Benchmark and the AIM Independent Resource Benchmark (Release 1.0)
File Server Mix

SUN SPARCserver 670 with Zitel CASD 2000

Price	CPU Type	Clock Rate	1st Level Cache	2nd Level Cache	RAM
N/A	SPARC	40 MHz	None	1 MB	64 MB

Disks	Disk Controllers	I/O Buffers	O/S	File System	Compiler
CASD 2000 2.0 GB, 64 MB Cache	SCSI-II	Dynamic	Solaris 2.2	UFS	GNU C

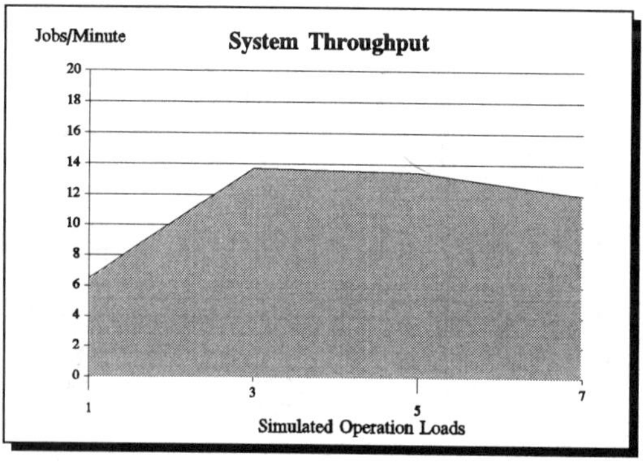

Peak Performance
13.7 AIM File Server Jobs/Minute
The **Peak Performance** reflects the system throughput at the point at which the system is able to process the most jobs per minute.

Sustained Performance
9.8 AIM File Server Loads
The **Sustained performance** indicates the multitasking operation load where the system's performance could become unacceptable, i.e. less than 1 job/minute/AIM File Server load.

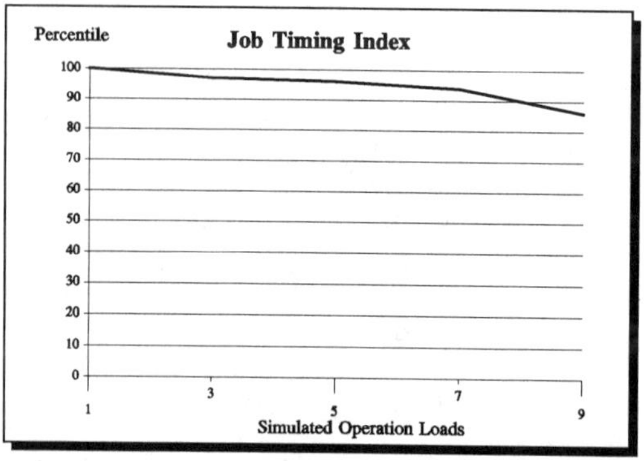

Job Timing Index
86 Percentile
The **Job Timing Index** is a measure of difference in completion times for concurrent jobs. It reveals the ability of a system to run processes simultaneously.

Certified By:

AIM Technology

Date: Dec 28, 1993
S/N# 0012

System Performance

When you are in the market for a new system, you want a top performer. You are also concerned about cost. When you have system specifications in hand, you are ready to do some comparison shopping. But there are so many vendors, and so many systems. Where do you start?

The goal of this guide is to take some of the legwork out of the shopping process. This section presents system performance information in three formats:

Price/Performance Guide

AIM Performance Reports

Buyer's Guide

Price / Performance Guide, pp. 18 - 31

The Price/Performance Guides use the prices and performance ratings from the AIM Certified Performance Reports to help you compare similar systems. Use this information to identify the systems that best meet the needs of your environment and budget.

Peak Performance vs. Sustained Performance: What Kind of Performance is Important to You?

AIM's ratings include one for peak performance and one for sustained performance. Both of these measurements are used in the price/ performance graphs. Use the measurement that is most meaningful in your environment.

A system's **peak performance** is the highest performance level that the system reaches under test. At a system's peak performance, an increase in the workload will cause a deterioration in performance. This rating is most applicable for processor-dependent applications (typically more prevalent on workstations).

A system's **sustained performance** is the performance level that a system attains when it is tested under heavy system loads. This rating shows the capacity of the system under heavy multitasking loads, where disk performance also becomes a significant factor.

When Do You Use The Peak Performance and Sustained Performance Graphs?

The Price/Peak Performance and Price/Sustained Performance graphs compare price and performance to calculate each system's performance value. The Peak Performance and Sustained Performance graphs compare performance only. When the price for a system varies from the price displayed in this guide, use your price and the information in the Peak Performance and Sustained Performance graphs to calculate your own performance value for the system.

How To Use the Graphs

There are six sets of graphs in the Price/Performance section. Each of the *first four sets* use six graphs to compare *system performance and price* in six price classes: Under $15,000, $15,000-$25,000, $25,000-$50,000, $50,000-$100,000, $100,000 - $500,000, and Over $500,000. The *last two sets* use two graphs to compare *performance* of Single-CPU, RISC systems, and Single-CPU, Intel Architecture.

When You Are Concerned About....	Use The Following Graphs...	Description
Price and occasional periods of heavy usage by one or more users	Best Price/Peak Performance	Identify systems that reach their peak performance for the least cost.
Price and periods of heavy usage	Best Price/Sustained Performance	Identify systems that reach their maximum capacity for the least cost.
Occasional periods of heavy usage by one or more users	Best Peak Performance	Identify the systems that are exceptionally powerful during occasional periods of heavy usage by one or more users.
Periods of heavy usage	Best Sustained Performance	Identify systems that maintain high performance under heavy system loads.
Performance of single-CPU RISC systems	Best Single-CPU RISC Performance	Identify the top performers in both peak performance and sustained performance categories.
Performance of single-CPU systems, Intel Architecture	Best Single-CPU Performance, Intel Architecture	Identify the top performers in both peak performance and sustained performance categories.

AIM Performance Reports, pp. 32 - 69

This part of the System Performance section presents brief excerpts from all new or updated AIM Performance Reports published since the last issue of the Price Performance Guide.

Note that reports are deleted from this guide when they are over one year old.

Understanding The AIM Ratings

The AIM Performance Report is developed using AIM's own state-of-the-art suite of benchmarks to evaluate computer system performance. Unlike many popular benchmarks that just measure singletasking CPU and/or floating point operation, AIM's benchmarks test total system performance of all major system components in a multitasking environment, including CPU, floating point, memory, disk, system calls, and function calls.

The benchmarks used to develop the AIM Performance Report (AIM System Benchmark - Suite III and AIM Subsystem Benchmark - Suite II) use five primary criteria to evaluate and rate systems:

- Peak performance (**AIM Performance Rating**)
- User loads (**Maximum User Loads**)
- Utilities (**Utilities Index**)
- Throughput (**Throughput Graph**)
- Price

The following paragraphs describe the ratings that AIM develops during the evaluation process and tell you how to use the ratings to select the system that best meets the needs of your environment.

AIM Performance Rating

A standard unit of measure for peak performance established by AIM Technology.

The use of a standard unit allows comparison between a wide range of systems, for example, a system rated at 30 AIMs is 50% more powerful in peak performance than a system rated at 20 AIMs.

The AIM Performance Rating identifies the maximum performance of the system under optimum usage of CPU, floating point, and disk caching. That is, the rating identifies the system's highest performance level when a significant amount of CPU, floating point, and disk caching is used.

This rating is important when evaluating all systems but is particularly applicable to workstations because many workstations process applications that are dependent on CPU, floating point, and disk caching.

Maximum User Load Rating

Tells you when performance can become unacceptable.

This rating identifies system capacity. If disk usage is significant in your environment (for example, multitasking workstations or multiuser systems), use this rating to find out how well the system performs under increasingly heavy workloads.

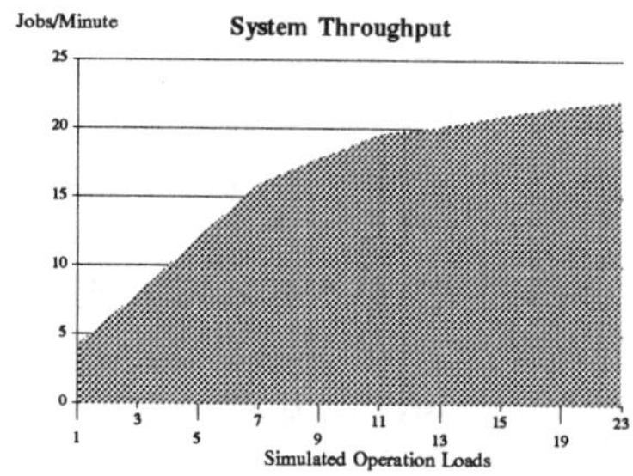

Utilities Index (MPH)

Reveals how well the system performs standard UNIX utilities.

If UNIX utilities are used to a significant degree in your environment, use this rating to evaluate how a system performs under heavy UNIX utilities usage.

Throughput Graph

Shows performance under various system loads.

Use this graph to find out if the system's performance is consistent under different workloads, and to evaluate system performance at workloads other than those identified by the AIM Performance Rating and the Maximum User Load Rating. When you are evaluating the performance of several systems, compare the throughput graphs to see how each handles a steadily increasing workload.

Price

Used for cost analysis.

When the price is used in conjunction with other ratings, the price identifies the system's performance value. For example, when you use the AIM Performance Rating and price to evaluate peak performance (price divided by total AIMs), you identify the cost/AIM.

If your price varies from the price quoted on the AIM Performance Report, use the ratings to calculate your own performance value for the system.

Complete Reports Available

Complete 4-page performance reports for all systems in this guide are available from AIM Technology. In addition to the information displayed in this section, the complete reports include the following UNIX performance data in graphical format:

PERFORMANCE AREA	DESCRIPTION
Disk	Disk performance is important for database applications, file servers, and software development.
Floating Point	Floating point performance is important for scientific and graphics applications.
Integer Math	Important for financial applications.
RAM Operations (Copy, Read/Write, Array)	RAM performance is important for desktop publishing and financial applications.
System Calls	create/close, fork, sbrk(), signal, and umask() are key UNIX performance parameters in the areas of file and process creation, memory allocation, signal processing, and file security.
Function Calls	Important for large, modular applications.

Buyer's Guide, pp. 70 - 112

This part of the System Performance section presents a **quick reference guide to systems from 28 major manufacturers.** The information in this section, extracted from AIM's Performance Reports, includes the following AIM-certified performance results:

- AIM Performance Rating (Peak)
- Maximum User Load Rating (Sustained)

Refer to the previous section for an explanation of the ratings.

Systems appear in alphabetical order. Note that reports are removed from this guide when they are over one year old. However, information on "out of print" systems or back issues of this guide are still available from AIM, or from system manufacturers, subject to availability.

Different configurations of the same system can produce *drastically* different performance results. To understand what factors are under evaluation, each system represented contains thorough hardware and software configuration information, along with the system's list price.

Best Price/Peak Performance

Systems that reach their peak performance for the least cost.

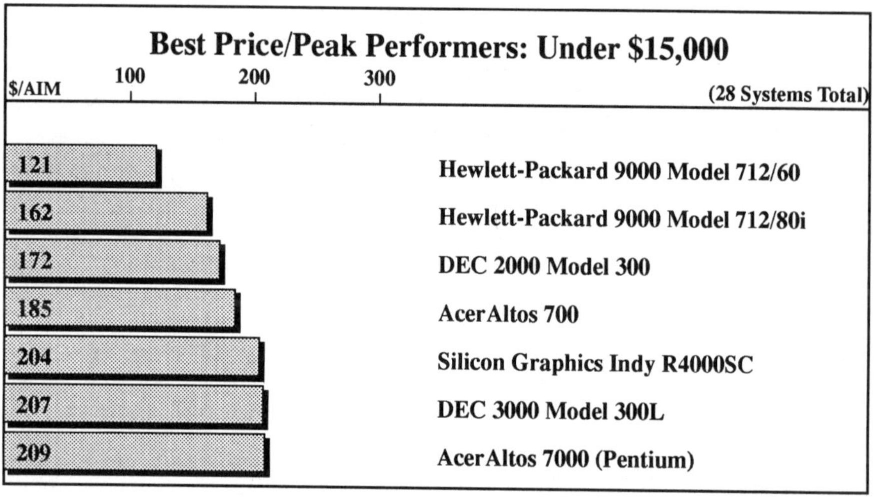

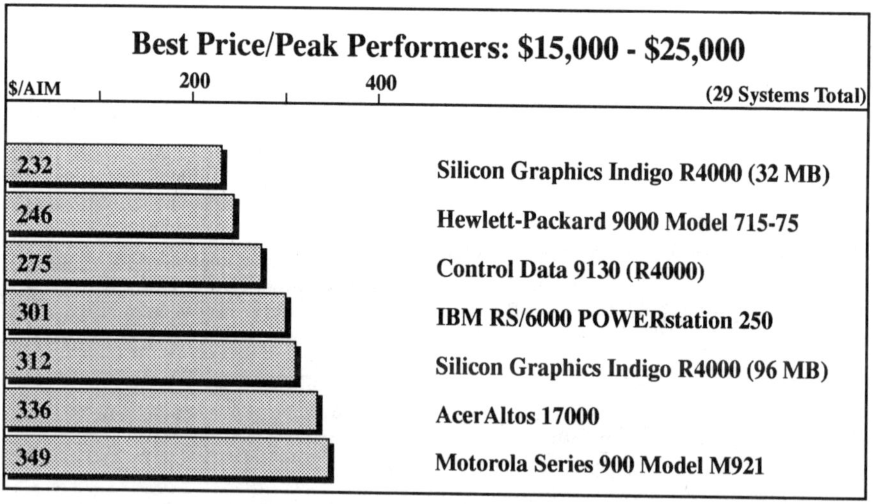

Best Price/Peak Performance

Systems that reach their peak performance for the least cost.

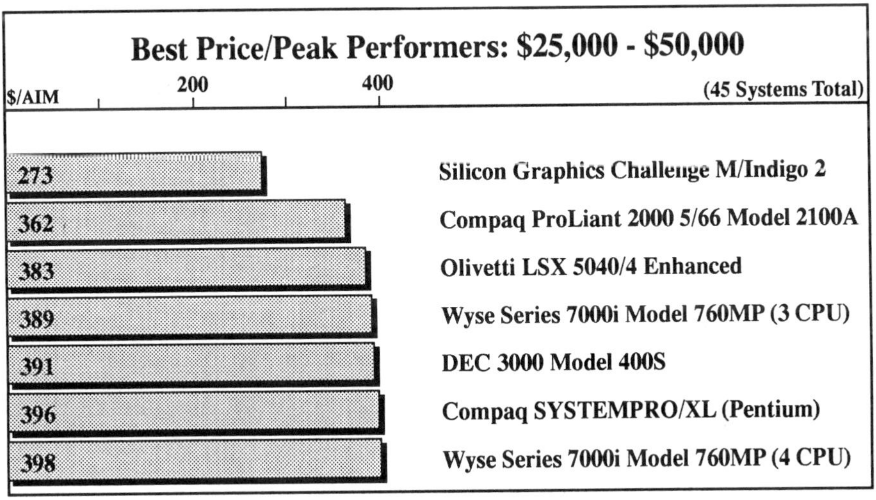

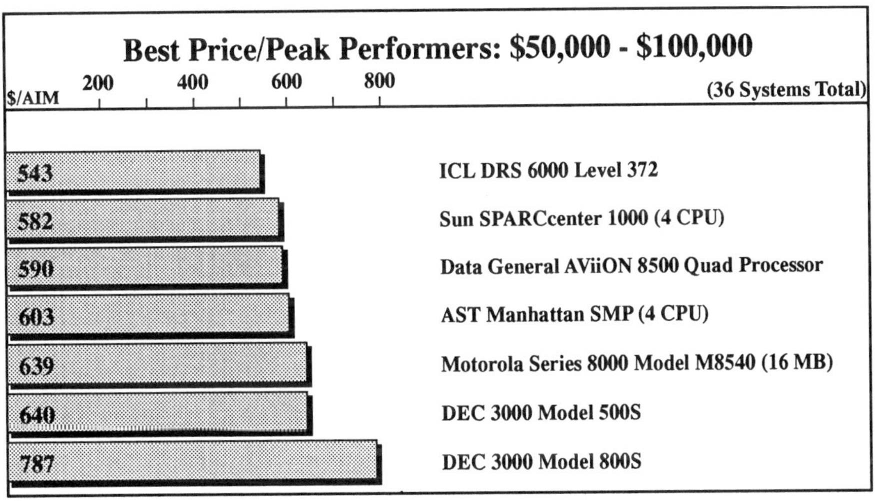

Best Price/Peak Performance

Systems that reach their peak performance for the least cost.

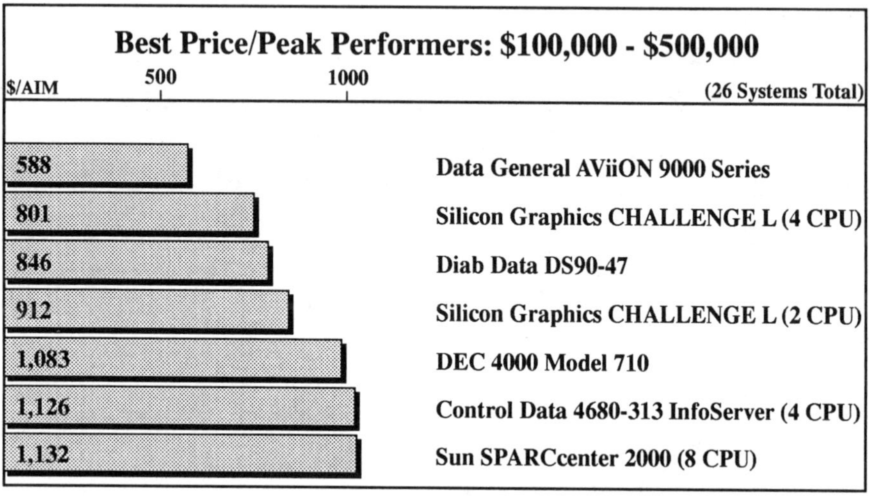

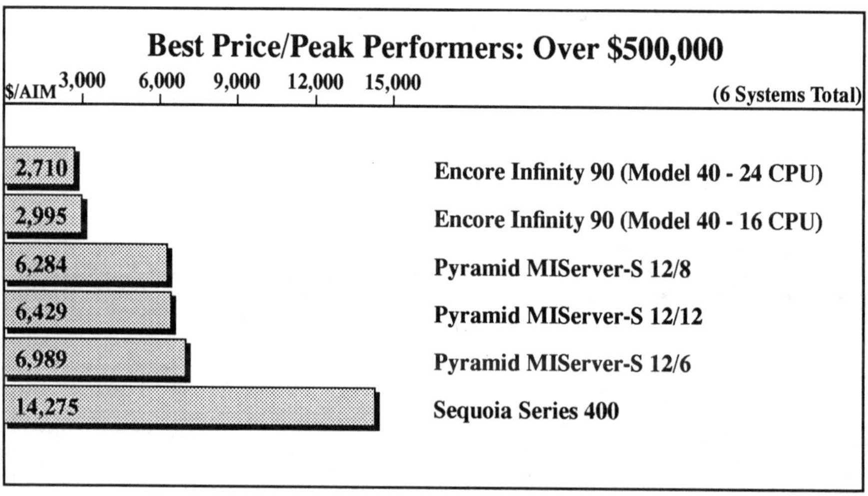

Best Price/Sustained Performance

Systems that reach their maximum capacity for the least cost

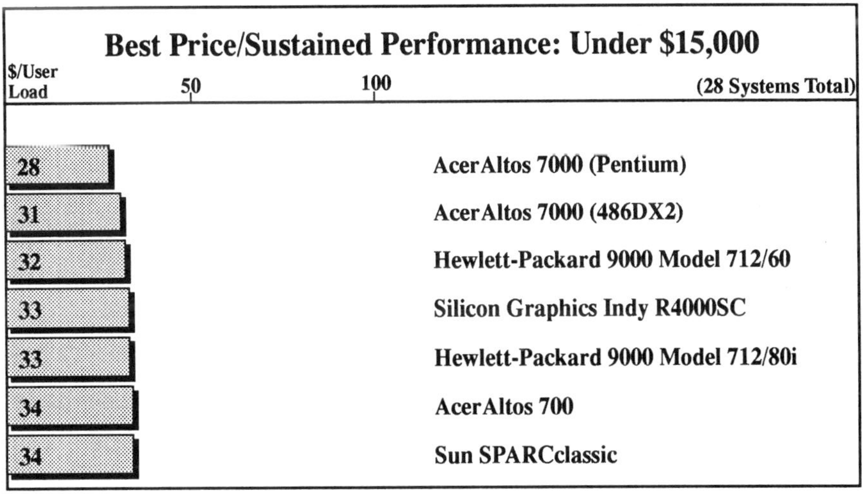

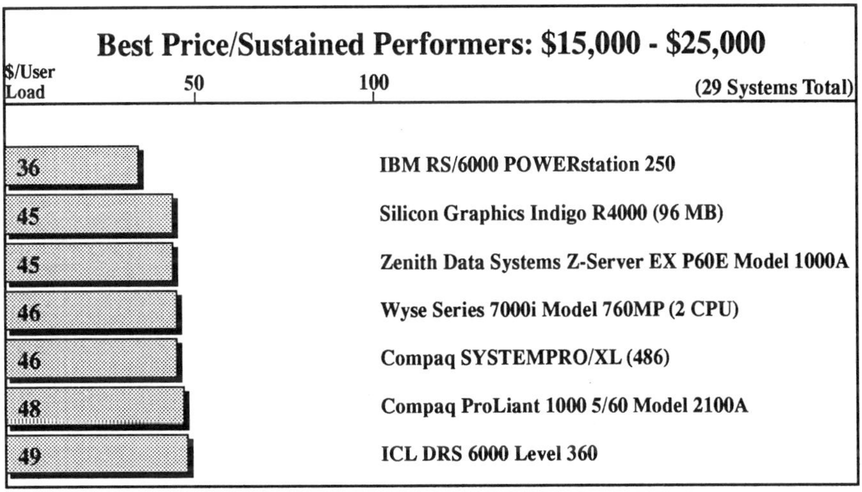

Best Price/Sustained Performance

Systems that reach their maximum capacity for the least cost.

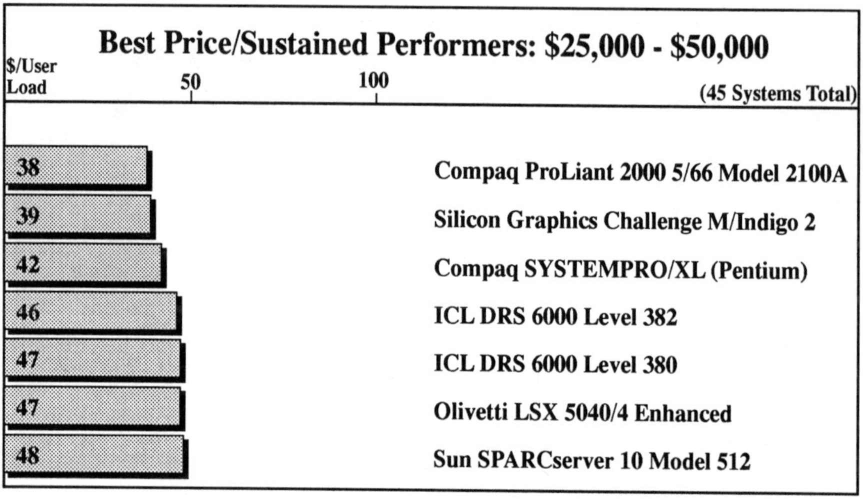

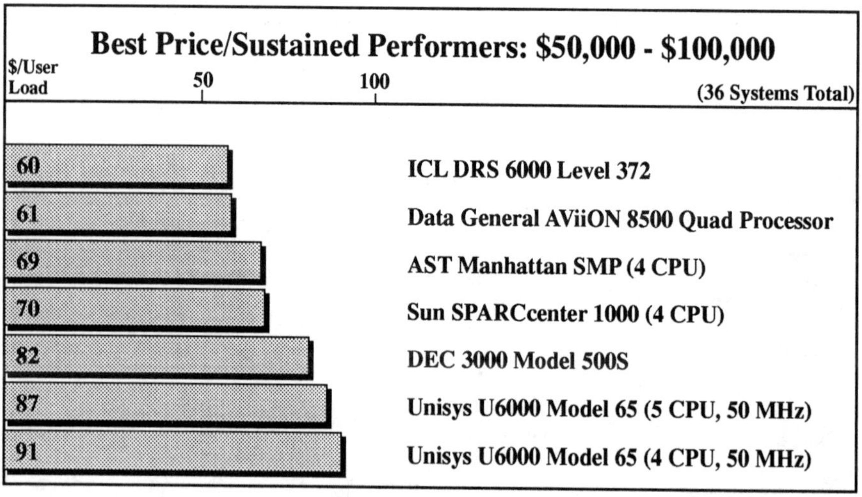

Best Price/Sustained Performance

Systems that reach their maximum capacity for the least cost.

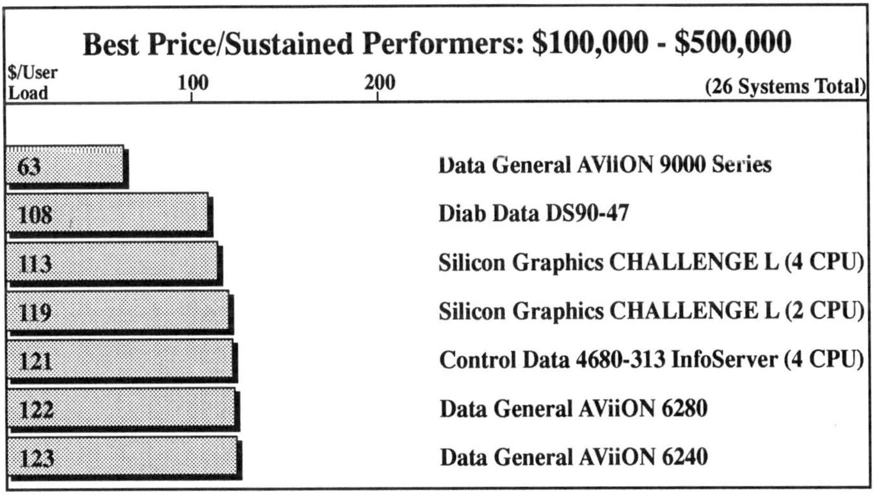

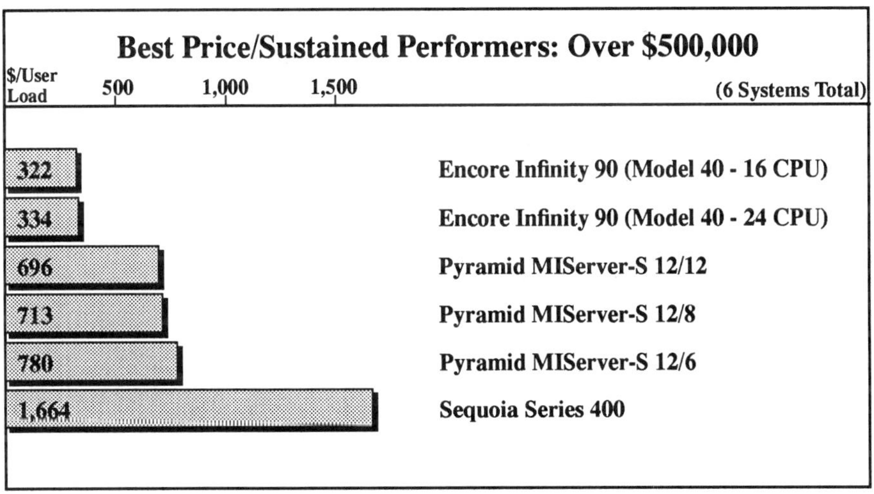

Best Peak Performance

Systems that are exceptionally powerful under light usage.

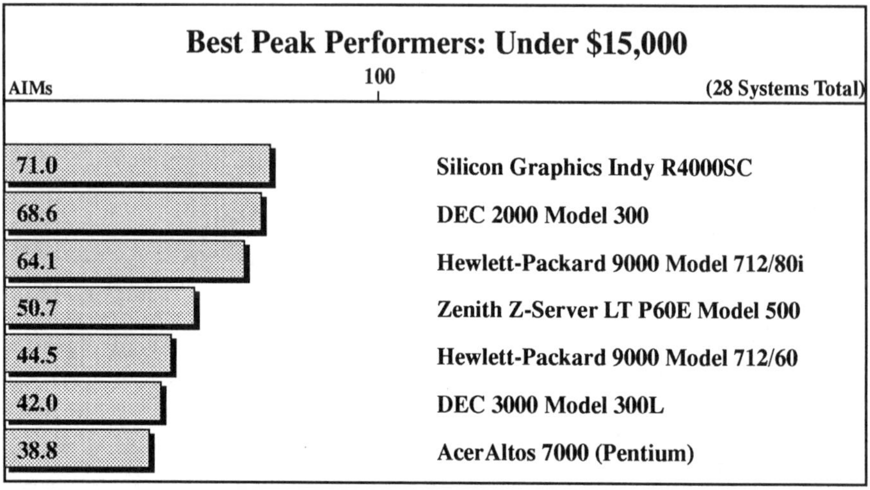

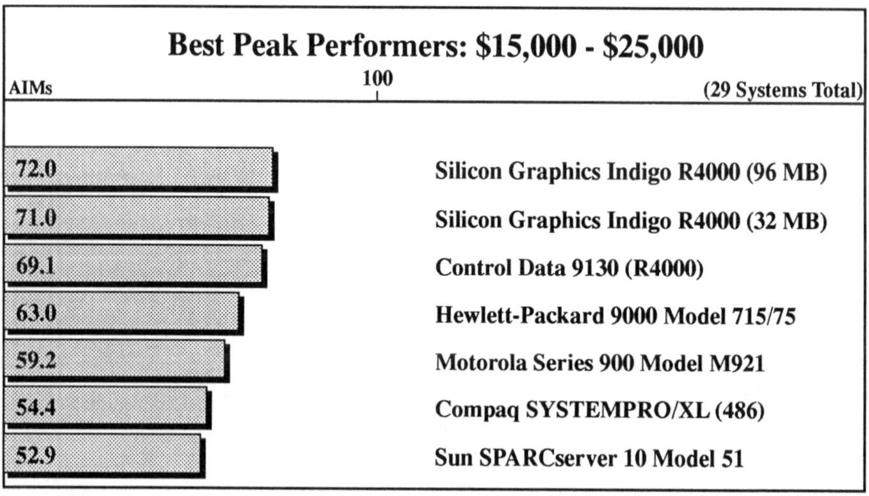

Best Peak Performance

Systems that are exceptionally powerful under light usage.

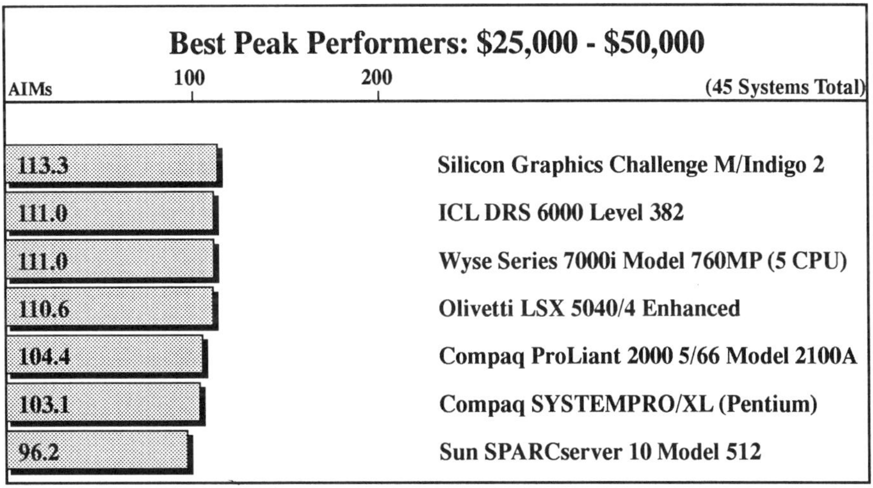

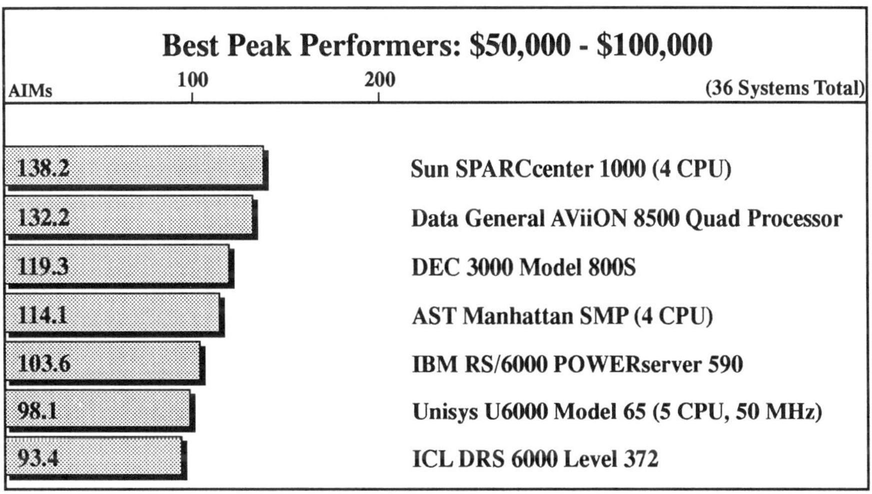

Best Peak Performance

Systems that are exceptionally powerful under light usage.

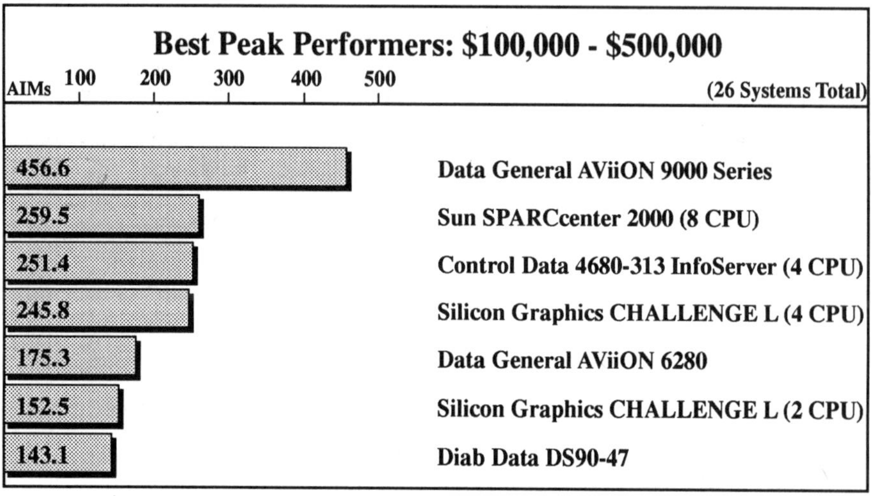

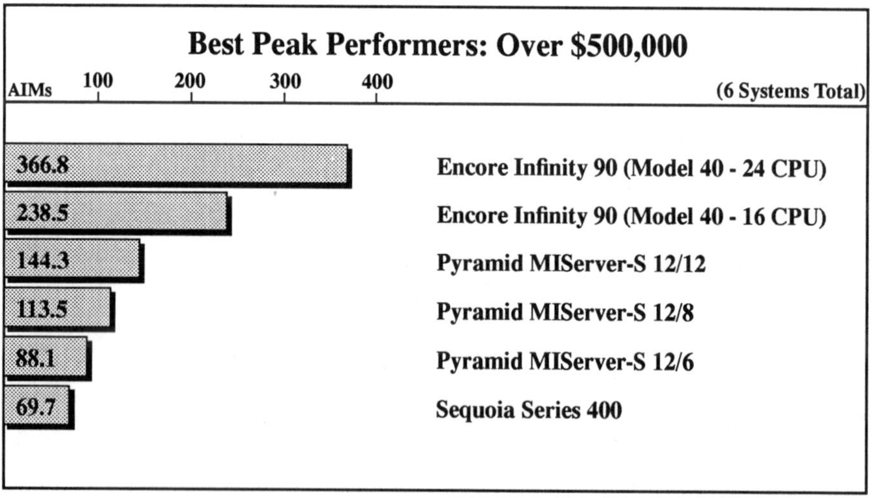

Best Sustained Performance

Systems that maintain high performance under heavy system loads.

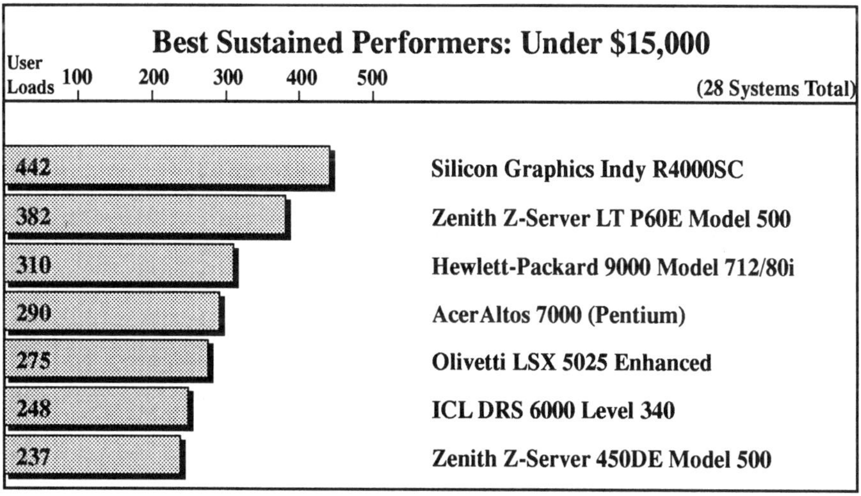

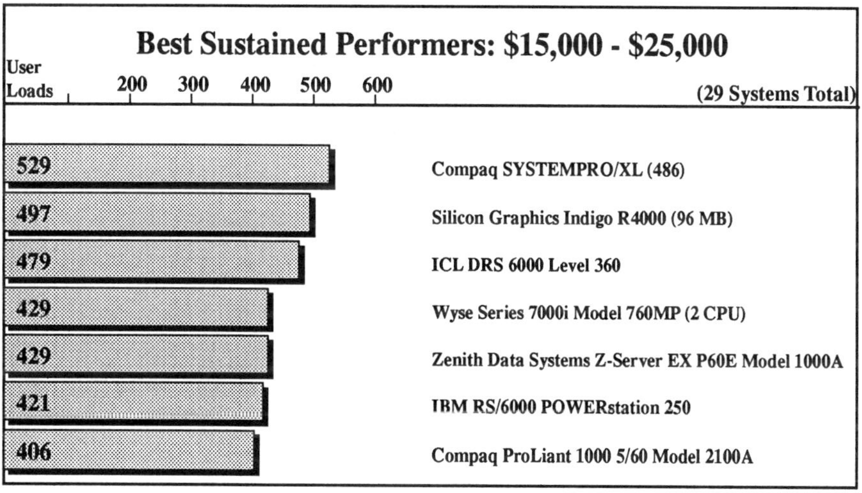

Best Sustained Performance

Systems that maintain high performance under heavy system loads.

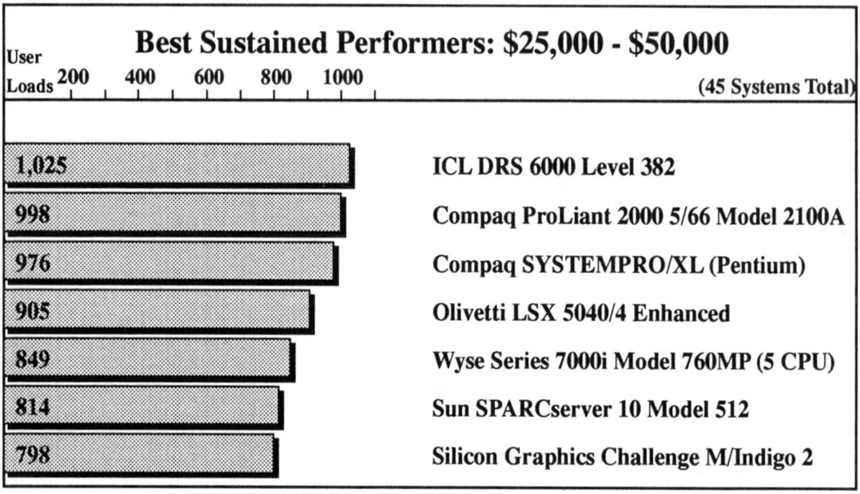

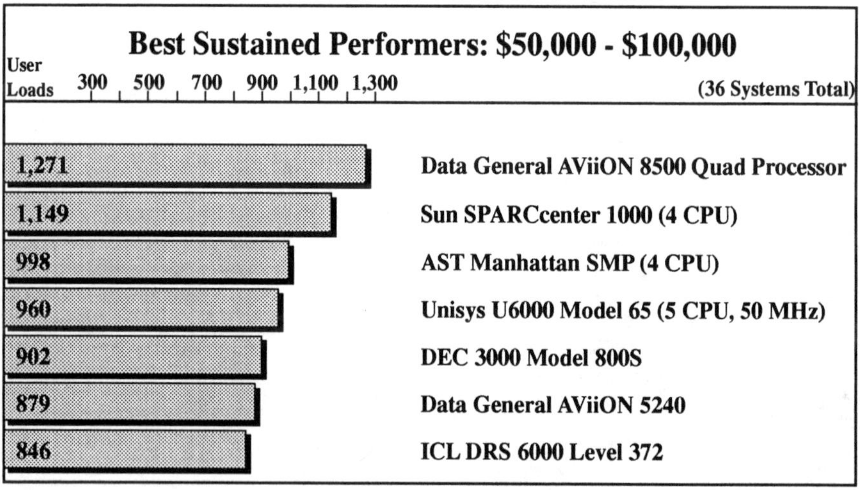

Best Sustained Performance

Systems that maintain high performance under heavy system loads.

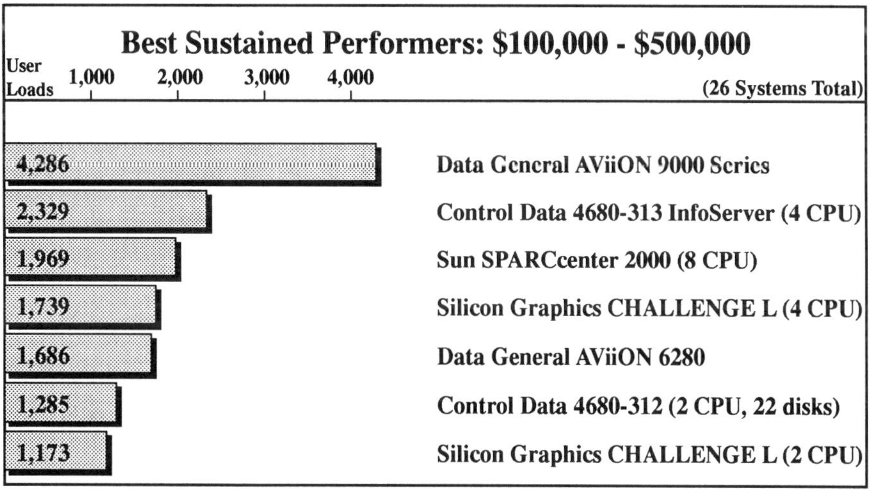

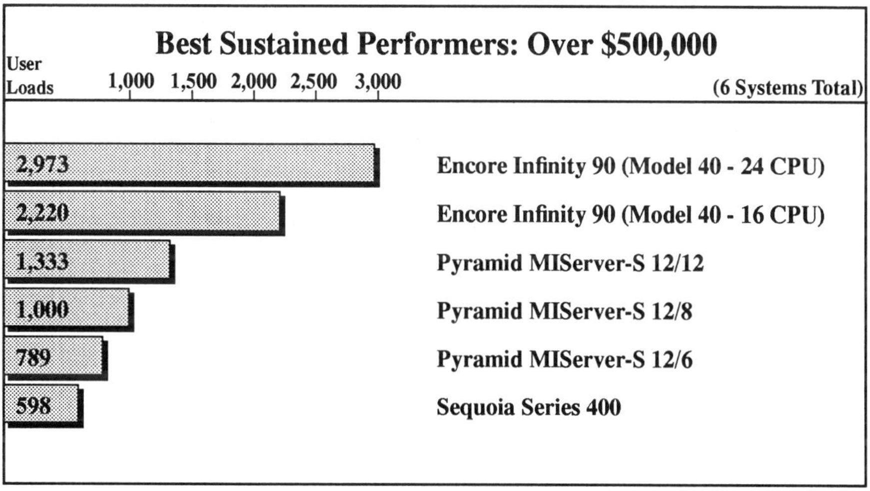

Best Single-CPU RISC Performance

Top performers in both peak performance and sustained performance categories.

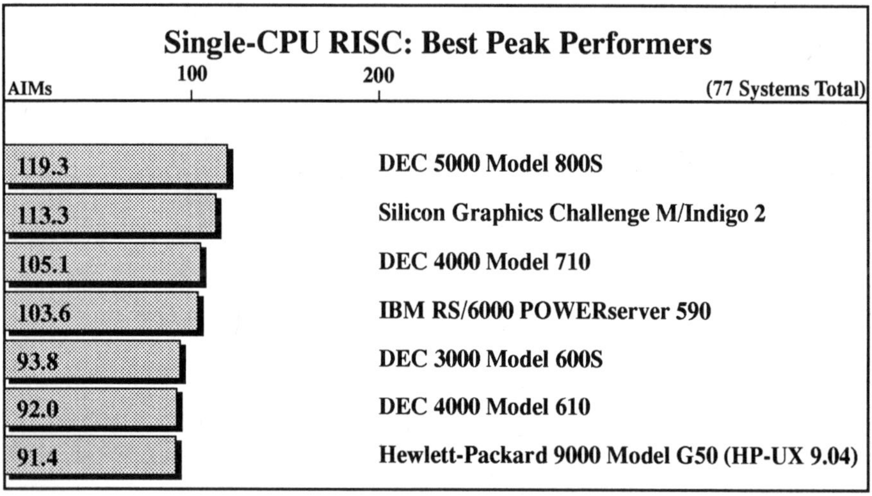

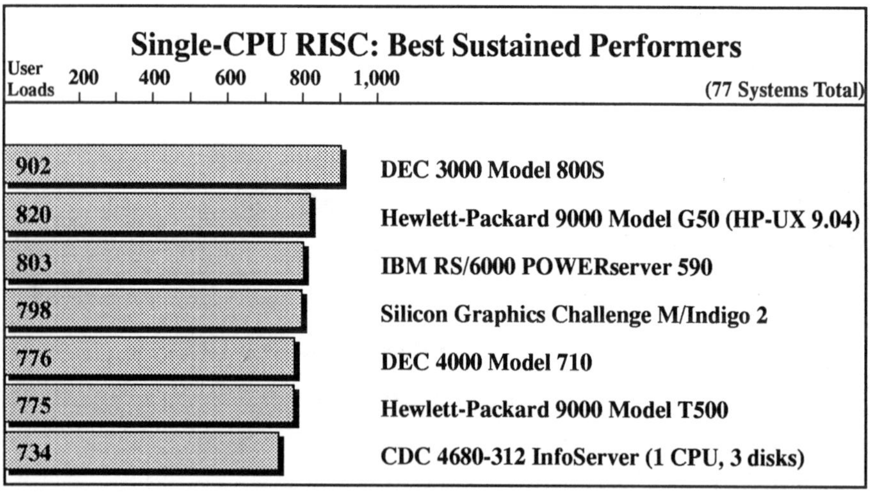

Best Single-CPU Performance

Intel Architecture

Top performers in both peak performance and sustained performance categories.

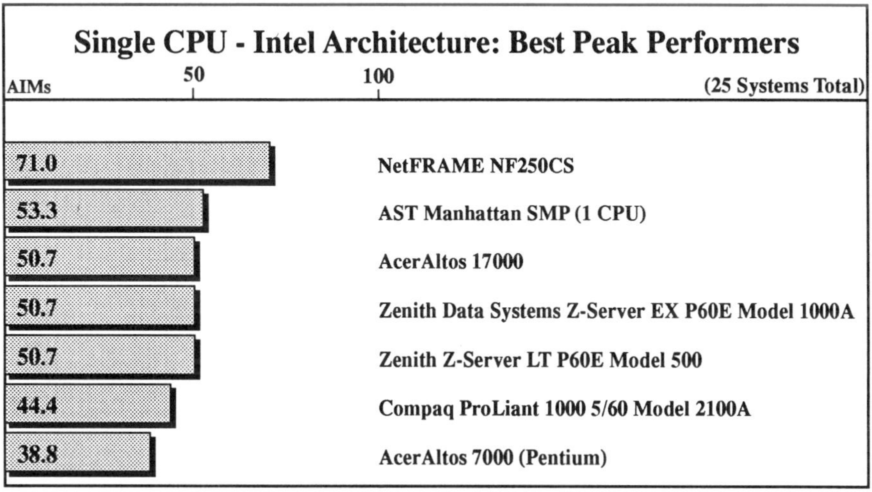

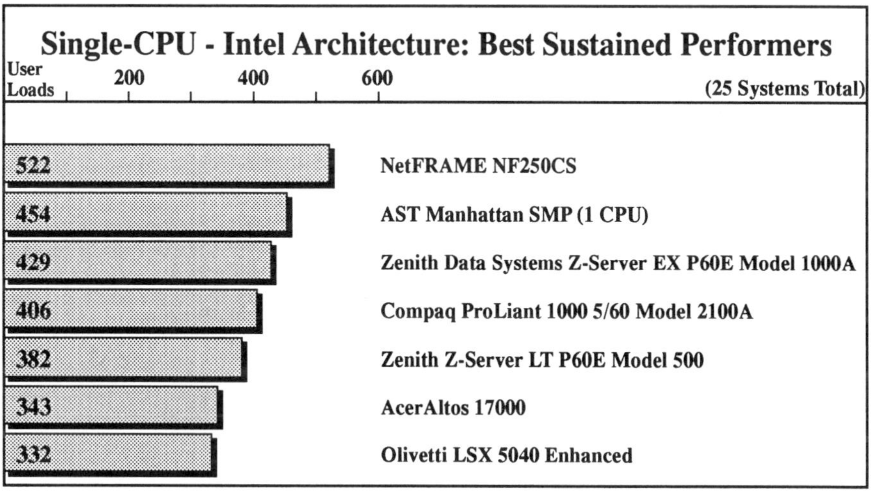

AIM Performance Report II

A UNIX Performance Summary Based on the AIM Benchmarks

AcerAltos 700

Price	*Cpu Type*	*Clock Rate*	*Ext. Cpu Cache*	*Floating Point*	*RAM*
$4,800	486DX2-66	66/33 MHz	128K 2nd lvl	Integrated	16 MB

Disks	*Disk Controllers*	*I/O Buffers*	*O/S*	*File System*	*Compiler*
520 MB, 12ms (3)	Adaptec 6360 SCSI	6960 KB	Altos/SCO UNIX 4.1b	EAFS	Metaware High C v2.32

AIM Performance Rating

25.9 AIMs

The **AIM Performance Rating** reflects the peak performance of this system measured in AIM Multiuser Performance Units. A VAX 11/780 typically rates 1 AIM. Performance Ratings of a wide range of UNIX systems can be compared using available AIM Performance Reports.

Maximum User Load

141 User Loads

The **Maximum User Load** indicates the multitasking user load where the system's performance could become unacceptable, i.e. less than 1 job/minute/user load.

Utilities Index

Utilities Missing

Miles per Hour (MPH) is the number of *Milestone* User Loads that this system completes per hour. Milestone exercises selected UNIX utilities as foreground and background tasks at moderate user loads.

System Throughput is the total amount of work the system processes, measured in jobs per minute.

Maximum Throughput is the point at which the system is able to process the most jobs per minute.

The system throughput for varying user load levels is presented at right ⇒

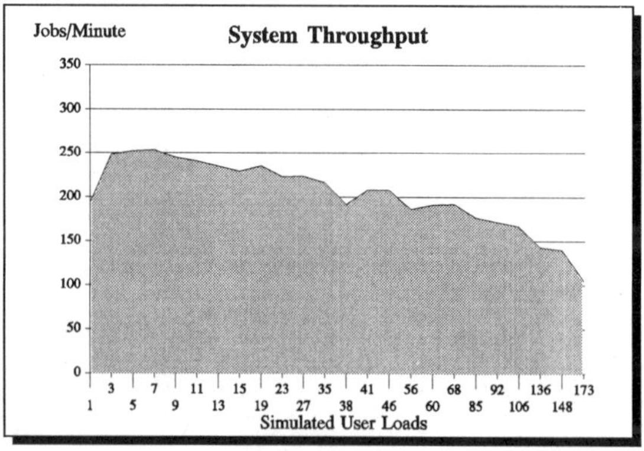

Maximum Throughput

253.8 Jobs/Minute

AIM UNIX SYSTEM PRICE PERFORMANCE GUIDE ONE FREE ISSUE TO QUALIFIED APPLICANTS

All questions must be answered. Incomplete forms will not be processed. Only applications that meet the publisher's qualification criteria will be accepted. Free offer available in U.S. and Canada only.

1. I WANT TO RECEIVE ONE FREE ISSUE OF THE AIM PRICE PERFORMANCE GUIDE

☐ Yes ☐ No

Name ____________________

Title ____________________

Company ____________________ Phone (____) ____________

Address ____________________

City ____________________ State ____________ Zip ____________

Signature ____________________ Date ____________

2. MY ORGANIZATION IS PRIMARILY: (check one only)

☐ 1 Manufacturer (computer systems)
☐ 2 Manufacturer (other related hardware)
☐ 3 System Integrator, VAR, Reseller
☐ 4 End User
☐ 5 Other (please specify) ____________

3. WHICH BEST DESCRIBES YOUR JOB FUNCTION? (check one only)

☐ 1 Computer systems Operations
☐ 2 Systems Design/Integration
☐ 3 Systems Analyst/Technical Support
☐ 4 Presales Systems Analyst
☐ 5 Development/Engineering
☐ 6 Sales/Marketing
☐ 7 Corporate/Administration
☐ 8 Market Research/Journalist
☐ 9 Consulting/Education
☐ 10 Other (please specify) ____________

4. MY ORGANIZATION PLANS TO PURCHASE THE FOLLOWING NUMBER OF UNIX COMPUTERS IN THE NEXT 12 MONTHS: (check one only)

☐ A none
☐ B 1-10
☐ C 11-50
☐ D 51-100
☐ E over 100

5. THE PURCHASES ABOVE WILL INCLUDE THE FOLLOWING TYPES OF UNIX-BASED COMPUTERS: (check all that apply)

☐ 1 Personal/PC
☐ 2 Workstation
☐ 3 X Terminal
☐ 4 Network File Server
☐ 5 Multiuser System
☐ 6 Other (please specify) ____________

6. I PERSONALLY USE BENCHMARKS AND/OR BENCHMARK RESULTS IN THE FOLLOWING WAYS: (check all that apply)

☐ 1 Potential Vendor Selection
☐ 2 Procurement Specification
☐ 3 Acceptance Testing
☐ 4 Design/Engineering
☐ 5 Performance Testing
☐ 6 Competitive Analysis
☐ 7 Proposal/Bid Response

PLEASE TURN OVER FORM AND COMPLETE QUESTIONS V123193

7. **PLEASE INDICATE YOUR EXPERIENCE WITH THE FOLLOWING SOURCES OF BENCHMARKS AND BENCHMARK DATA: (check all that apply)**

	Previously Used	Plan Future Use
1 AIM Technology	☐	☐
2 Neal Nelson Associates	☐	☐
3 RTE Commercial Supplier	☐	☐
4 SPEC	☐	☐
5 TPC	☐	☐
6 Public Domain	☐	☐
7 Trade Press	☐	☐
8 In-house developed	☐	☐

9 Other (please specify) ______________________________

8. **I WOULD LIKE TO SEE THE FOLLOWING MANUFACTURERS/MODELS INCLUDED IN THE NEXT UNIX SYSTEM PRICE PERFORMANCE GUIDE**

Manufacturer	Model
______________	______________
______________	______________

9. **I AM PERSONALLY INVOLVED IN THE USE, SELECTION, OR APPROVAL OF UNIX-BASED NETWORK MANAGEMENT TOOLS** ☐ Yes ☐ No

10a. **I WOULD BE INTERESTED IN APPLICATION SOFTWARE PERFORMANCE ON VARIOUS VENDOR PLATFORMS FOR THE FOLLOWING APPLICATIONS: (check all that apply)**

☐ 1. Accounting
☐ 2. Word processing
☐ 3. Spreadsheet
☐ 4. Database
☐ 5. CAD/CAE
☐ 6. Desktop publishing
☐ 7. Software development

10b. **TOP 3 APPLICATIONS THAT I USE:** ______________________________

____

PLEASE FOLD ALONG THIS LINE. DO NOT TAPE OR STAPLE

NO POSTAGE NECESSARY IF MAILED IN THE UNITED STATES

BUSINESS REPLY MAIL

FIRST CLASS MAIL PERMIT NO. 1033 SANTA CLARA, CA

POSTAGE WILL BE PAID BY ADDRESSEE

AIM TECHNOLOGY
4699 Old Ironsides Drive, Suite 150
Santa Clara, CA 95054-9718

AIM Performance Report II

A UNIX Performance Summary Based on the AIM Benchmarks

AcerAltos 7000

Price	*Cpu Type*	*Clock Rate*	*Ext. Cpu Cache*	*Floating Point*	*RAM*
$7,006	486DX2	33/66 MHz	256K	Integrated	64 MB
Disks	*Disk Controllers*	*I/O Buffers*	*O/S*	*File System*	*Compiler*
520 MB, 12ms (3)	Adaptec 7770 SCSI II	32768 KB	Altos/SCO UNIX 4.1b	EAFS	Metaware High C v2.32

AIM Performance Rating

26.9 AIMs

The **AIM Performance Rating** reflects the peak performance of this system measured in AIM Multiuser Performance Units. A VAX 11/780 typically rates 1 AIM. Performance Ratings of a wide range of UNIX systems can be compared using available AIM Performance Reports.

Maximum User Load

225 User Loads

The **Maximum User Load** indicates the multitasking user load where the system's performance could become unacceptable, i.e. less than 1 job/minute/user load.

Utilities Index

Utilities Missing

Miles per Hour (MPH) is the number of *Milestone* User Loads that this system completes per hour. Milestone exercises selected UNIX utilities as foreground and background tasks at moderate user loads.

System Throughput is the total amount of work the system processes, measured in jobs per minute.

Maximum Throughput is the point at which the system is able to process the most jobs per minute.

The system throughput for varying user load levels is presented at right ⇒

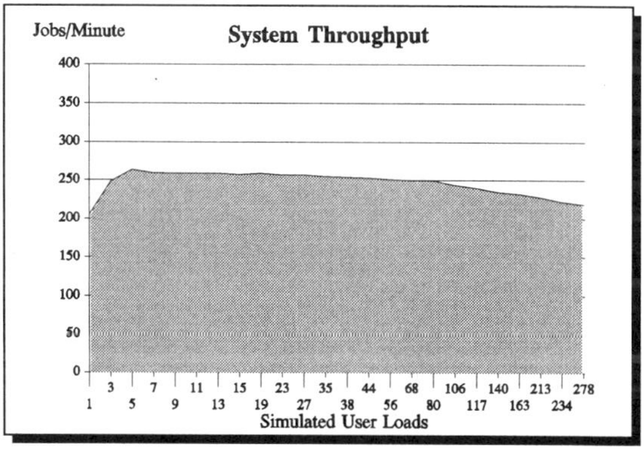

Maximum Throughput

263.6 Jobs/Minute

AIM Performance Report II

A UNIX Performance Summary Based on the AIM Benchmarks

AcerAltos 7000

Price	Cpu Type	Clock Rate	Ext. Cpu Cache	Floating Point	RAM
$8,106	Pentium	33 MHz	512K 2nd lvl	Integrated	64 MB

Disks	Disk Controllers	I/O Buffers	O/S	File System	Compiler
520 MB, 12ms (3)	Adaptec 7770 SCSI II	32768 KB	Altos/SCO UNIX 4.1b	EAFS	SCO C Compiler v1.1.4

AIM Performance Rating

38.8 AIMs

The **AIM Performance Rating** reflects the peak performance of this system measured in AIM Multiuser Performance Units. A VAX 11/780 typically rates 1 AIM. Performance Ratings of a wide range of UNIX systems can be compared using available AIM Performance Reports.

Maximum User Load

290 User Loads

The **Maximum User Load** indicates the multitasking user load where the system's performance could become unacceptable, i.e. less than 1 job/minute/user load.

Utilities Index

Utilities Missing

Miles per Hour (MPH) is the number of *Milestone* User Loads that this system completes per hour. Milestone exercises selected UNIX utilities as foreground and background tasks at moderate user loads.

System Throughput is the total amount of work the system processes, measured in jobs per minute.

Maximum Throughput is the point at which the system is able to process the most jobs per minute.

The system throughput for varying user load levels is presented at right ⇒

Maximum Throughput

380.6 Jobs/Minute

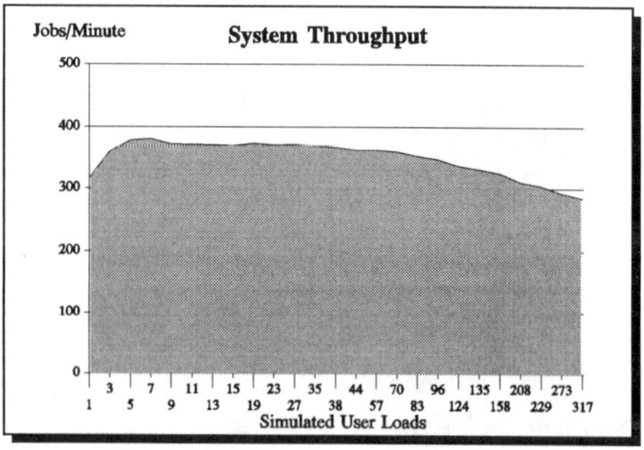

AIM Performance Report II

A UNIX Performance Summary Based on the AIM Benchmarks

AcerAltos 17000

Price	*Cpu Type*	*Clock Rate*	*Ext. Cpu Cache*	*Floating Point*	*RAM*
$17,025	Pentium	60 MHz	256K	Integrated	64 MB

Disks	*Disk Controllers*	*I/O Buffers*	*O/S*	*File System*	*Compiler*
520 MB, 12ms (4)	SCA II SCSI	32 MB	Altos/SCO UNIX 4.1b	EAFS	SCO C Compiler v1.1.4

AIM Performance Rating

50.7 AIMs

The **AIM Performance Rating** reflects the peak performance of this system measured in AIM Multiuser Performance Units. A VAX 11/780 typically rates 1 AIM. Performance Ratings of a wide range of UNIX systems can be compared using available AIM Performance Reports.

Maximum User Load

343 User Loads

The **Maximum User Load** indicates the multitasking user load where the system's performance could become unacceptable, i.e. less than 1 job/minute/user load.

Utilities Index

Utilities Missing

Miles per Hour (MPH) is the number of *Milestone* User Loads that this system completes per hour. Milestone exercises selected UNIX utilities as foreground and background tasks at moderate user loads.

System Throughput is the total amount of work the system processes, measured in jobs per minute.

Maximum Throughput is the point at which the system is able to process the most jobs per minute.

The system throughput for varying user load levels is presented at right ⇒

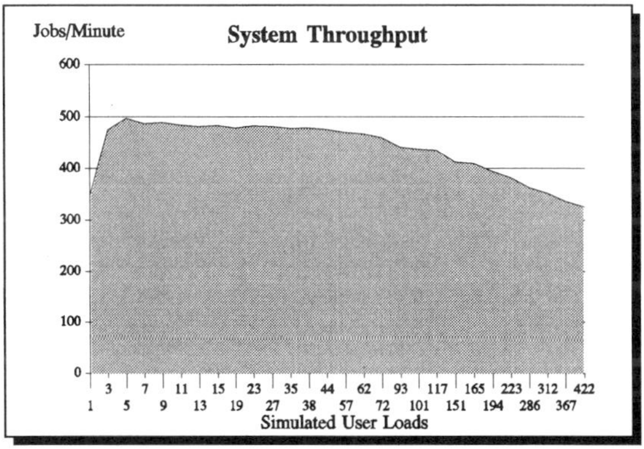

Maximum Throughput

497.1 Jobs/Minute

AIM Performance Report II

A UNIX Performance Summary Based on the AIM Benchmarks

Apple Workgroup Server 95

Price	*Cpu Type*	*Clock Rate*	*Ext. Cpu Cache*	*Floating Point*	*RAM*
$6,648	68040	33 MHz	256K	Integrated	32 MB

Disks	*Disk Controllers*	*I/O Buffers*	*O/S*	*File System*	*Compiler*
500 MB, 12ms 230 MB, 16ms	NCR 53C96 SCSI	Dynamic	A/UX 3.0.2	BSD/UFS	c89 v1.1

AIM Performance Rating

22.2 AIMs

The **AIM Performance Rating** reflects the peak performance of this system measured in AIM Multiuser Performance Units. A VAX 11/780 typically rates 1 AIM. Performance Ratings of a wide range of UNIX systems can be compared using available AIM Performance Reports.

Maximum User Load

137 User Loads

The **Maximum User Load** indicates the multitasking user load where the system's performance could become unacceptable, i.e. less than 1 job/minute/user load.

Utilities Index

Utilities Unsuccessful

Miles per Hour (MPH) is the number of *Milestone* User Loads that this system completes per hour. Milestone exercises selected UNIX utilities as foreground and background tasks at moderate user loads.

System Throughput is the total amount of work the system processes, measured in jobs per minute.

Maximum Throughput is the point at which the system is able to process the most jobs per minute.

The system throughput for varying user load levels is presented at right ⇒

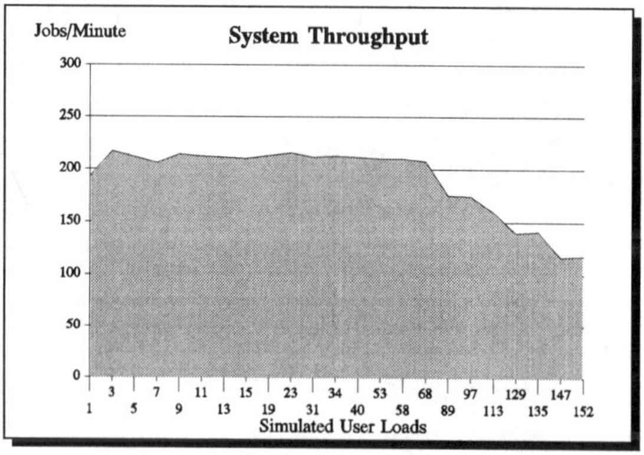

Maximum Throughput

217.5 Jobs/Minute

AIM Performance Report II

A UNIX Performance Summary Based on the AIM Benchmarks

Control Data 9130 (R4000)

Price	Cpu Type	Clock Rate	Ext. Cpu Cache	Floating Point	RAM
$18,995	R4000 SC	50/100 MHz	8K inst, 8K data, 1M 2nd	Integrated	32 MB
Disks	**Disk Controllers**	**I/O Buffers**	**O/S**	**File System**	**Compiler**
1.0 GB, 12ms	Integrated SCSI	Dynamic	IRIX 5.1.0.1	EFS	MIPS C v3.17

AIM Performance Rating

69.1 AIMs

The **AIM Performance Rating** reflects the peak performance of this system measured in AIM Multiuser Performance Units. A VAX 11/780 typically rates 1 AIM. Performance Ratings of a wide range of UNIX systems can be compared using available AIM Performance Reports.

Maximum User Load

160 User Loads

The **Maximum User Load** indicates the multitasking user load where the system's performance could become unacceptable, i.e. less than 1 job/minute/user load.

Utilities Index

Utilities Missing

Miles per Hour (MPH) is the number of *Milestone* User Loads that this system completes per hour. Milestone exercises selected UNIX utilities as foreground and background tasks at moderate user loads.

System Throughput is the total amount of work the system processes, measured in jobs per minute.

Maximum Throughput is the point at which the system is able to process the most jobs per minute.

The system throughput for varying user load levels is presented at right ⇒

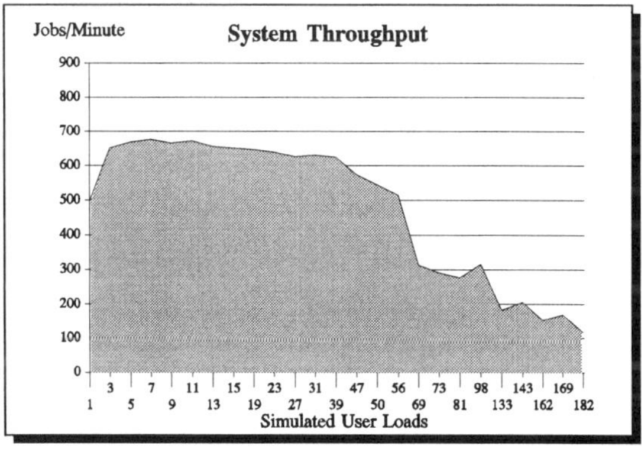

Maximum Throughput

676.7 Jobs/Minute

AIM Performance Report II

A UNIX Performance Summary Based on the AIM Benchmarks

Data General AViiON 9000 Series

Price	*Cpu Type*	*Clock Rate*	*Ext. Cpu Cache*	*Floating Point*	*RAM*
$268,551	88110-L5 (8)	50 MHz	8K data/8K inst 1st 1 MB/cpu 2nd	Integrated	608 MB
Disks	***Disk Controllers***	***I/O Buffers***	***O/S***	***File System***	***Compiler***
520 MB, 8.5ms (4)	Integrated SCSI	Dynamic	DG/UX 5.4R3.00	DG/UX	Gnu C 2.4.5

AIM Performance Rating

456.6 AIMs

The **AIM Performance Rating** reflects the peak performance of this system measured in AIM Multiuser Performance Units. A VAX 11/780 typically rates 1 AIM. Performance Ratings of a wide range of UNIX systems can be compared using available AIM Performance Reports.

Maximum User Load

4286 User Loads

The **Maximum User Load** indicates the multitasking user load where the system's performance could become unacceptable, i.e. less than 1 job/minute/user load.

Utilities Index

Utilities Missing

Miles per Hour (MPH) is the number of *Milestone* User Loads that this system completes per hour. Milestone exercises selected UNIX utilities as foreground and background tasks at moderate user loads.

System Throughput is the total amount of work the system processes, measured in jobs per minute.

Maximum Throughput is the point at which the system is able to process the most jobs per minute.

The system throughput for varying user load levels is presented at right ⇒

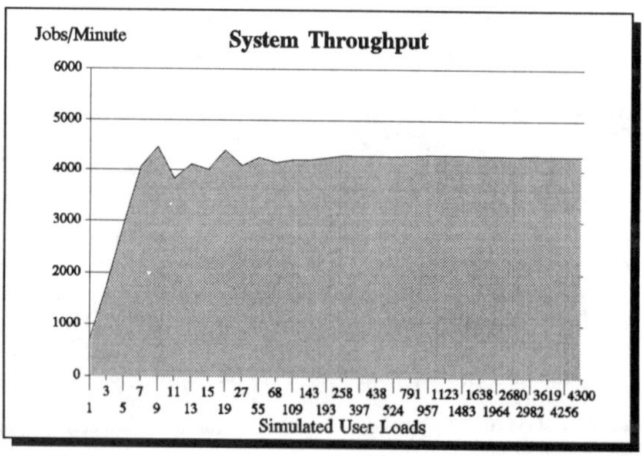

Maximum Throughput

4474.3 Jobs/Minute

AIM Performance Report II

A UNIX Performance Summary Based on the AIM Benchmarks

DEC 2000 Model 300

Price	Cpu Type	Clock Rate	Ext. Cpu Cache	Floating Point	RAM
$11,798	21064	150 MHz	64 KB	Integrated	64 MB

Disks	Disk Controllers	I/O Buffers	O/S	File System	Compiler
1.3 GB, 9ms (2)	SCSI	Dynamic	DEC OSF/1 V1.3b	UFS	DEC OSF/1 AXP C V1.3

AIM Performance Rating

68.6 AIMs

The **AIM Performance Rating** reflects the peak performance of this system measured in AIM Multiuser Performance Units. A VAX 11/780 typically rates 1 AIM. Performance Ratings of a wide range of UNIX systems can be compared using available AIM Performance Reports.

Maximum User Load

178 User Loads

The **Maximum User Load** indicates the multitasking user load where the system's performance could become unacceptable, i.e. less than 1 job/minute/user load.

Utilities Index

Utilities Missing

Miles per Hour (MPH) is the number of *Milestone* User Loads that this system completes per hour. Milestone exercises selected UNIX utilities as foreground and background tasks at moderate user loads.

System Throughput is the total amount of work the system processes, measured in jobs per minute.

Maximum Throughput is the point at which the system is able to process the most jobs per minute.

The system throughput for varying user load levels is presented at right ⇒

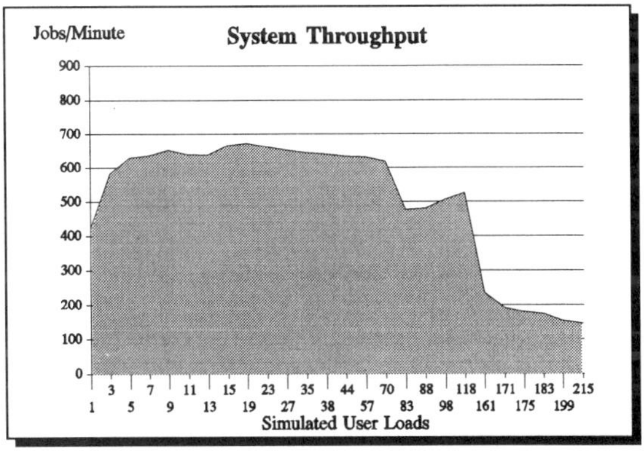

Maximum Throughput

672.5 Jobs/Minute

AIM Performance Report II

A UNIX Performance Summary Based on the AIM Benchmarks

DEC 3000 Model 300L

Price	*Cpu Type*	*Clock Rate*	*Ext. Cpu Cache*	*Floating Point*	*RAM*
$8,695	21064	100 MHz	256K	Integrated	64 MB

Disks	*Disk Controllers*	*I/O Buffers*	*O/S*	*File System*	*Compiler*
1.3 GB, 9ms	Integrated SCSI	Dynamic	DEC OSF/1 X1.3 (Rev 10.411)	UFS	DEC OSF/1 AXP C X1.3.0308

AIM Performance Rating

42 AIMs

The **AIM Performance Rating** reflects the peak performance of this system measured in AIM Multiuser Performance Units. A VAX 11/780 typically rates 1 AIM. Performance Ratings of a wide range of UNIX systems can be compared using available AIM Performance Reports.

Maximum User Load

225 User Loads

The **Maximum User Load** indicates the multitasking user load where the system's performance could become unacceptable, i.e. less than 1 job/minute/user load.

Utilities Index

Utilities Missing

Miles per Hour (MPH) is the number of *Milestone* User Loads that this system completes per hour. Milestone exercises selected UNIX utilities as foreground and background tasks at moderate user loads.

System Throughput is the total amount of work the system processes, measured in jobs per minute.

Maximum Throughput is the point at which the system is able to process the most jobs per minute.

The system throughput for varying user load levels is presented at right ⇒

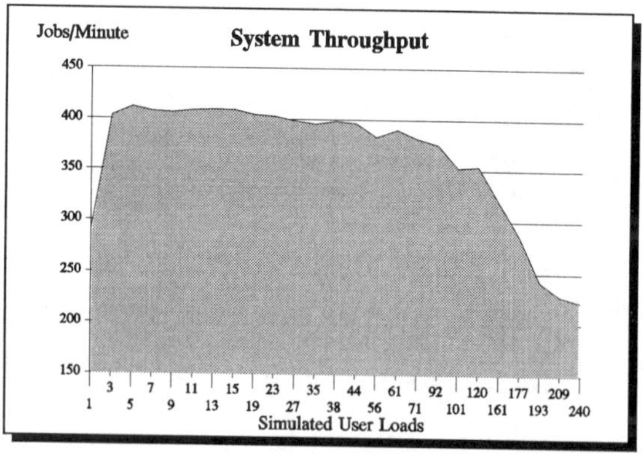

Maximum Throughput

411.7 Jobs/Minute

AIM Performance Report II

A UNIX Performance Summary Based on the AIM Benchmarks

DEC 3000 Model 400S

Price	Cpu Type	Clock Rate	Ext. Cpu Cache	Floating Point	RAM
$27,504	21064	133 MHz	512K	Integrated	128 MB

Disks	Disk Controllers	I/O Buffers	O/S	File System	Compiler
1.3 GB, 9.5ms (2) 426 MB, 14ms	Int SCSI + SCSI	Dynamic	DEC OSF/1 V1.2 (Rev 9)	UFS	DEC C v3.11

AIM Performance Rating

70.3 AIMs

The **AIM Performance Rating** reflects the peak performance of this system measured in AIM Multiuser Performance Units. A VAX 11/780 typically rates 1 AIM. Performance Ratings of a wide range of UNIX systems can be compared using available AIM Performance Reports.

Maximum User Load

485 User Loads

The **Maximum User Load** indicates the multitasking user load where the system's performance could become unacceptable, i.e. less than 1 job/minute/user load.

Utilities Index

Utilities Missing

Miles per Hour (MPH) is the number of *Milestone* User Loads that this system completes per hour. Milestone exercises selected UNIX utilities as foreground and background tasks at moderate user loads.

System Throughput is the total amount of work the system processes, measured in jobs per minute.

Maximum Throughput is the point at which the system is able to process the most jobs per minute.

The system throughput for varying user load levels is presented at right ⇒

Maximum Throughput

688.7 Jobs/Minute

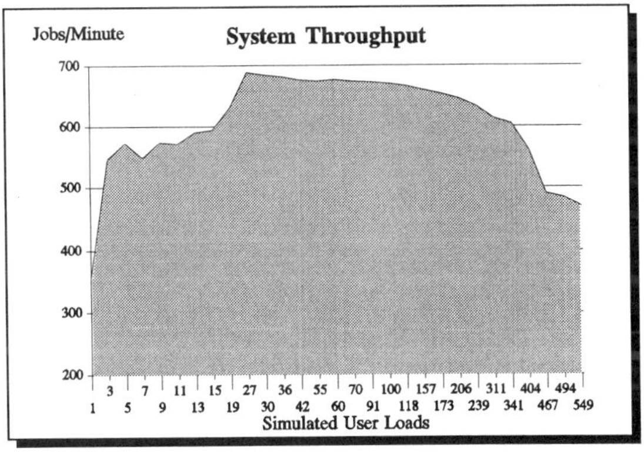

AIM Performance Report II

A UNIX Performance Summary Based on the AIM Benchmarks

DEC 3000 Model 500S

Price	*Cpu Type*	*Clock Rate*	*Ext. Cpu Cache*	*Floating Point*	*RAM*
$53,088	21064	150 MHz	512K	Integrated	192 MB

Disks	*Disk Controllers*	*I/O Buffers*	*O/S*	*File System*	*Compiler*
1.3 GB, 9ms(2) 426 MB, 14.5ms(6)	Integrated SCSI (2)	Dynamic + 1M PrestoServe	DEC OSF/1 V1.2 (Rev 9)	UFS	DEC C v3.11

AIM Performance Rating

82.9 AIMs

The **AIM Performance Rating** reflects the peak performance of this system measured in AIM Multiuser Performance Units. A VAX 11/780 typically rates 1 AIM. Performance Ratings of a wide range of UNIX systems can be compared using available AIM Performance Reports.

Maximum User Load

649 User Loads

The **Maximum User Load** indicates the multitasking user load where the system's performance could become unacceptable, i.e. less than 1 job/minute/user load.

Utilities Index

Utilities Missing

Miles per Hour (MPH) is the number of *Milestone* User Loads that this system completes per hour. Milestone exercises selected UNIX utilities as foreground and background tasks at moderate user loads.

System Throughput is the total amount of work the system processes, measured in jobs per minute.

Maximum Throughput is the point at which the system is able to process the most jobs per minute.

The system throughput for varying user load levels is presented at right ⇒

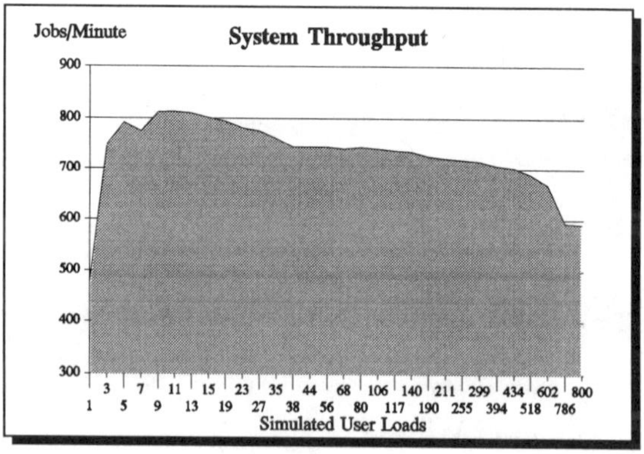

Maximum Throughput

812.9 Jobs/Minute

AIM Performance Report II

A UNIX Performance Summary Based on the AIM Benchmarks

DEC 3000 Model 600S

Price	*Cpu Type*	*Clock Rate*	*Ext. Cpu Cache*	*Floating Point*	*RAM*
$38,609	21064	175 MHz	2 MB	Integrated	128 MB

Disks	*Disk Controllers*	*I/O Buffers*	*O/S*	*File System*	*Compiler*
1.3 GB, 9ms (3)	SCSI (2)	Dynamic	DEC OSF/1 T2.0-2 (Rev 146)	UFS	DEC OSF/1 AXP C T2.0

AIM Performance Rating

93.8 AIMs

The **AIM Performance Rating** reflects the peak performance of this system measured in AIM Multiuser Performance Units. A VAX 11/780 typically rates 1 AIM. Performance Ratings of a wide range of UNIX systems can be compared using available AIM Performance Reports.

Maximum User Load

537 User Loads

The **Maximum User Load** indicates the multitasking user load where the system's performance could become unacceptable, i.e. less than 1 job/minute/user load.

Utilities Index

Utilities Missing

Miles per Hour (MPH) is the number of *Milestone* User Loads that this system completes per hour. Milestone exercises selected UNIX utilities as foreground and background tasks at moderate user loads.

System Throughput is the total amount of work the system processes, measured in jobs per minute.

Maximum Throughput is the point at which the system is able to process the most jobs per minute.

The system throughput for varying user load levels is presented at right ⇒

Maximum Throughput

919.2 Jobs/Minute

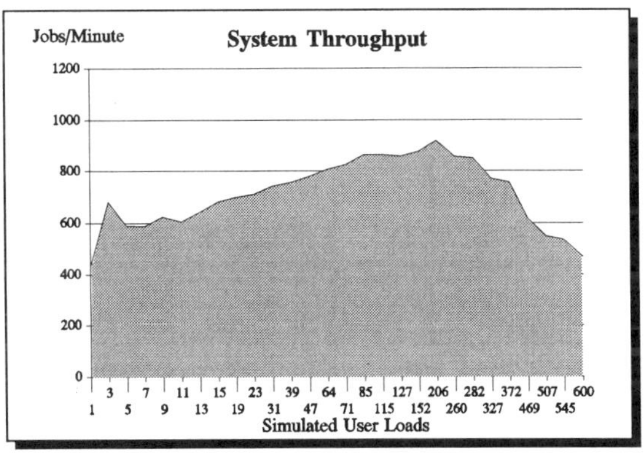

AIM Performance Report II

A UNIX Performance Summary Based on the AIM Benchmarks

DEC 3000 Model 800S

Price	Cpu Type	Clock Rate	Ext. Cpu Cache	Floating Point	RAM
$93,844	21064	200 MHz	2 MB	Integrated	384 MB

Disks	Disk Controllers	I/O Buffers	O/S	File System	Compiler
1.3 GB, 9ms (4)	SCSI (2)	Dynamic + 1 MB PrestoServe	DEC OSF/1 T2.0-2 (Rev 146)	UFS	DEC OSF/1 AXP C T2.0

AIM Performance Rating

119.3 AIMs

The **AIM Performance Rating** reflects the peak performance of this system measured in AIM Multiuser Performance Units. A VAX 11/780 typically rates 1 AIM. Performance Ratings of a wide range of UNIX systems can be compared using available AIM Performance Reports.

Maximum User Load

902 User Loads

The **Maximum User Load** indicates the multitasking user load where the system's performance could become unacceptable, i.e. less than 1 job/minute/user load.

Utilities Index

Utilities Missing

Miles per Hour (MPH) is the number of *Milestone* User Loads that this system completes per hour. Milestone exercises selected UNIX utilities as foreground and background tasks at moderate user loads.

System Throughput is the total amount of work the system processes, measured in jobs per minute.

Maximum Throughput is the point at which the system is able to process the most jobs per minute.

The system throughput for varying user load levels is presented at right ⇒

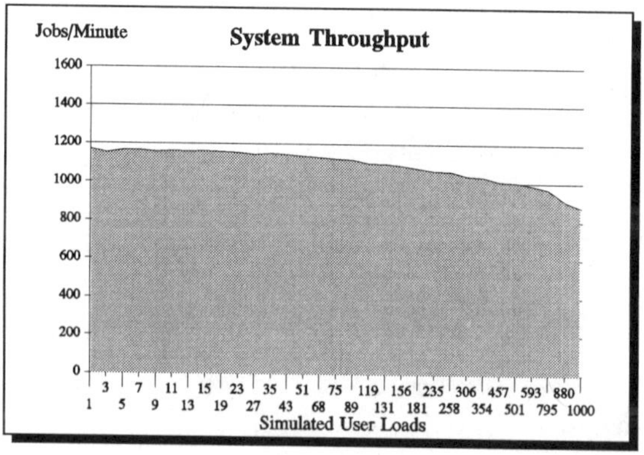

Maximum Throughput

1169.4 Jobs/Minute

AIM Performance Report II

A UNIX Performance Summary Based on the AIM Benchmarks

DEC 4000 Model 610

Price	Cpu Type	Clock Rate	Ext. Cpu Cache	Floating Point	RAM
$94,776	21064	160 MHz	1 MB	Integrated	512 MB

Disks	Disk Controllers	I/O Buffers	O/S	File System	Compiler
1.3 GB, 9ms (3)	SCSI	Dynamic + 4 MB PrestoServe	DEC OSF/1 V1.3 (Rev 111)	UFS	DEC OSF/1 AXP C V1.3

AIM Performance Rating

92 AIMs

The **AIM Performance Rating** reflects the peak performance of this system measured in AIM Multiuser Performance Units. A VAX 11/780 typically rates 1 AIM. Performance Ratings of a wide range of UNIX systems can be compared using available AIM Performance Reports.

Maximum User Load

655 User Loads

The **Maximum User Load** indicates the multitasking user load where the system's performance could become unacceptable, i.e. less than 1 job/minute/user load.

Utilities Index

Utilities Missing

Miles per Hour (MPH) is the number of *Milestone* User Loads that this system completes per hour. Milestone exercises selected UNIX utilities as foreground and background tasks at moderate user loads.

System Throughput is the total amount of work the system processes, measured in jobs per minute.

Maximum Throughput is the point at which the system is able to process the most jobs per minute.

The system throughput for varying user load levels is presented at right ⇒

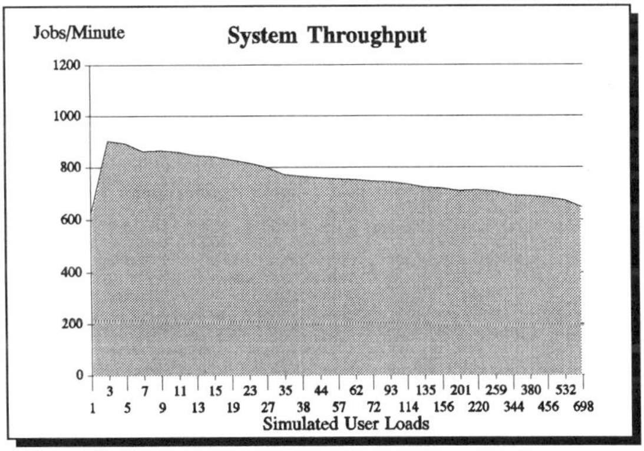

Maximum Throughput

901.7 Jobs/Minute

AIM Performance Report II

A UNIX Performance Summary Based on the AIM Benchmarks

DEC 4000 Model 710

Price	*Cpu Type*	*Clock Rate*	*Ext. Cpu Cache*	*Floating Point*	*RAM*
$113,848	21064	190 MHz	4 MB	Integrated	512 MB

Disks	*Disk Controllers*	*I/O Buffers*	*O/S*	*File System*	*Compiler*
1.3 GB, 9ms (3)	SCSI	Dynamic + 4 MB PrestoServe	DEC OSF/1 V1.3 (Rev 111)	UFS	DEC OSF/1 AXP C V1.3

AIM Performance Rating

105.1 AIMs

The **AIM Performance Rating** reflects the peak performance of this system measured in AIM Multiuser Performance Units. A VAX 11/780 typically rates 1 AIM. Performance Ratings of a wide range of UNIX systems can be compared using available AIM Performance Reports.

Maximum User Load

776 User Loads

The **Maximum User Load** indicates the multitasking user load where the system's performance could become unacceptable, i.e. less than 1 job/minute/user load.

Utilities Index

Utilities Missing

Miles per Hour (MPH) is the number of *Milestone* User Loads that this system completes per hour. Milestone exercises selected UNIX utilities as foreground and background tasks at moderate user loads.

System Throughput is the total amount of work the system processes, measured in jobs per minute.

Maximum Throughput is the point at which the system is able to process the most jobs per minute.

The system throughput for varying user load levels is presented at right ⇒

Maximum Throughput

1029.9 Jobs/Minute

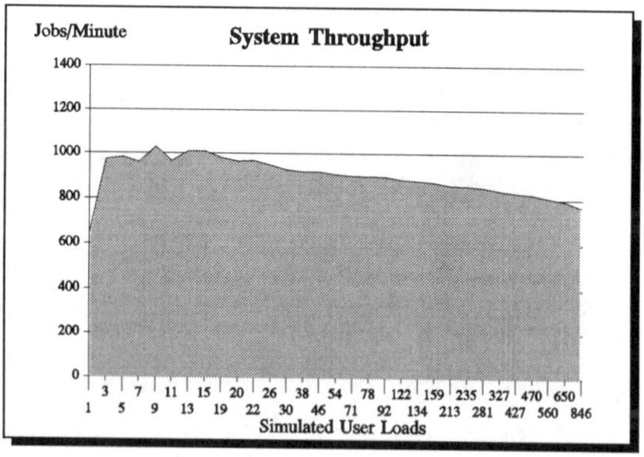

AIM Performance Report II

A UNIX Performance Summary Based on the AIM Benchmarks

Hewlett-Packard 9000 Model 712/60

Price	*Cpu Type*	*Clock Rate*	*Ext. Cpu Cache*	*Floating Point*	*RAM*
$5,400	PA 7100LC	60 MHz	64K	Integrated	16 MB

Disks	*Disk Controllers*	*I/O Buffers*	*O/S*	*File System*	*Compiler*
525 MB, 13ms	Integrated SCSI II	Dynamic	HP-UX 9.03	BFS	HP 92453 v10.03

AIM Performance Rating

44.5 AIMs

The **AIM Performance Rating** reflects the peak performance of this system measured in AIM Multiuser Performance Units. A VAX 11/780 typically rates 1 AIM. Performance Ratings of a wide range of UNIX systems can be compared using available AIM Performance Reports.

Maximum User Load

170 User Loads

The **Maximum User Load** indicates the multitasking user load where the system's performance could become unacceptable, i.e. less than 1 job/minute/user load.

Utilities Index

Utilities Missing

Miles per Hour (MPH) is the number of *Milestone* User Loads that this system completes per hour. Milestone exercises selected UNIX utilities as foreground and background tasks at moderate user loads.

System Throughput is the total amount of work the system processes, measured in jobs per minute.

Maximum Throughput is the point at which the system is able to process the most jobs per minute.

The system throughput for varying user load levels is presented at right →

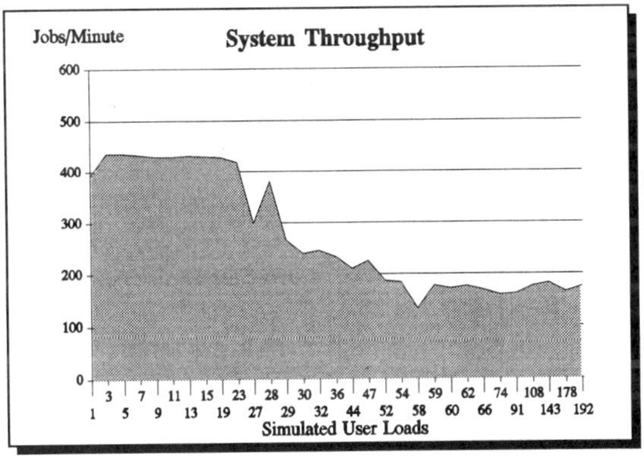

Maximum Throughput

435.9 Jobs/Minute

AIM Performance Report II

A UNIX Performance Summary Based on the AIM Benchmarks

Hewlett-Packard 9000 712/80i

Price	*Cpu Type*	*Clock Rate*	*Ext. Cpu Cache*	*Floating Point*	*RAM*
$10,380	PA7100LC	80 MHz	256K	Integrated	32 MB

Disks	*Disk Controllers*	*I/O Buffers*	*O/S*	*File System*	*Compiler*
1 GB, 11.5ms	Integrated SCSI-II	Dynamic	HP-UX 9.03	BFS	HP 92453 v10.03

AIM Performance Rating

64.1 AIMs

The **AIM Performance Rating** reflects the peak performance of this system measured in AIM Multiuser Performance Units. A VAX 11/780 typically rates 1 AIM. Performance Ratings of a wide range of UNIX systems can be compared using available AIM Performance Reports.

Maximum User Load

310 User Loads

The **Maximum User Load** indicates the multitasking user load where the system's performance could become unacceptable, i.e. less than 1 job/minute/user load.

Utilities Index

Utilities Missing

Miles per Hour (MPH) is the number of *Milestone* User Loads that this system completes per hour. Milestone exercises selected UNIX utilities as foreground and background tasks at moderate user loads.

System Throughput is the total amount of work the system processes, measured in jobs per minute.

Maximum Throughput is the point at which the system is able to process the most jobs per minute.

The system throughput for varying user load levels is presented at right ⇒

Maximum Throughput

628.4 Jobs/Minute

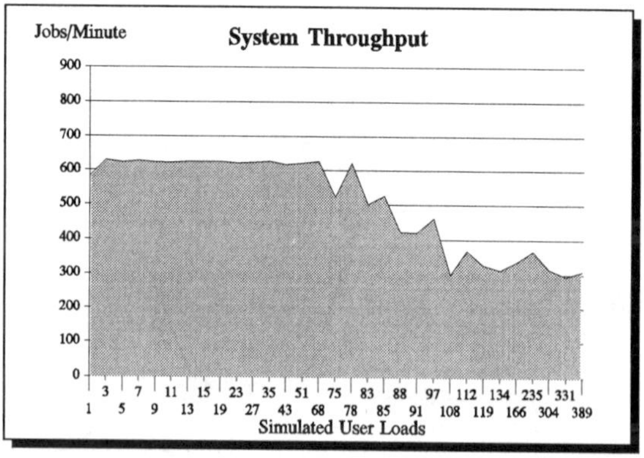

AIM Performance Report II

A UNIX Performance Summary Based on the AIM Benchmarks

Hewlett-Packard 9000 Series 700 Model 715/75

Price	*Cpu Type*	*Clock Rate*	*Ext. Cpu Cache*	*Floating Point*	*RAM*
$15,490	PA-RISC 7100	75 MHz	256K data, 256K inst	Integrated	32 MB

Disks	*Disk Controllers*	*I/O Buffers*	*O/S*	*File System*	*Compiler*
1.0 GB, 10ms	SCSI	Dynamic	HP-UX 9.01	HFS	HP C A.09.34

AIM Performance Rating

63 AIMs

The **AIM Performance Rating** reflects the peak performance of this system measured in AIM Multiuser Performance Units. A VAX 11/780 typically rates 1 AIM. Performance Ratings of a wide range of UNIX systems can be compared using available AIM Performance Reports.

Maximum User Load

125 User Loads

The **Maximum User Load** indicates the multitasking user load where the system's performance could become unacceptable, i.e. less than 1 job/minute/user load.

Utilities Index

Utilities Missing

Miles per Hour (MPH) is the number of *Milestone* User Loads that this system completes per hour. Milestone exercises selected UNIX utilities as foreground and background tasks at moderate user loads.

System Throughput is the total amount of work the system processes, measured in jobs per minute.

Maximum Throughput is the point at which the system is able to process the most jobs per minute.

The system throughput for varying user load levels is presented at right ⇒

Maximum Throughput

617.2 Jobs/Minute

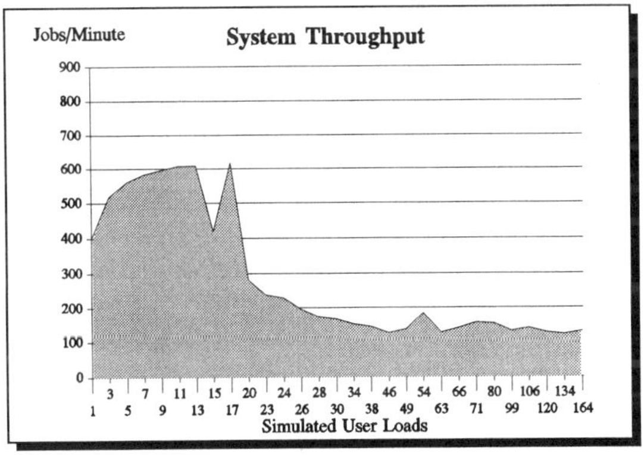

AIM Performance Report II

A UNIX Performance Summary Based on the AIM Benchmarks

Hewlett-Packard 9000 Model E25

Price	Cpu Type	Clock Rate	Ext. Cpu Cache	Floating Point	RAM
$44,494	PA-RISC 7100LC	48 MHz	64K	Integrated	128 MB

Disks	Disk Controllers	I/O Buffers	O/S	File System	Compiler
1.0 GB, 10.5ms (2) 1.0 GB, 10.5ms (7)	Internal SE SCSI HP-PB FW SCSI	64 MB	HP-UX 9.04	BSD	HP C X.10.03

AIM Performance Rating

44.5 AIMs

The **AIM Performance Rating** reflects the peak performance of this system measured in AIM Multiuser Performance Units. A VAX 11/780 typically rates 1 AIM. Performance Ratings of a wide range of UNIX systems can be compared using available AIM Performance Reports.

Maximum User Load

392 User Loads

The **Maximum User Load** indicates the multitasking user load where the system's performance could become unacceptable, i.e. less than 1 job/minute/user load.

Utilities Index

Utilities Missing

Miles per Hour (MPH) is the number of *Milestone* User Loads that this system completes per hour. Milestone exercises selected UNIX utilities as foreground and background tasks at moderate user loads.

System Throughput is the total amount of work the system processes, measured in jobs per minute.

Maximum Throughput is the point at which the system is able to process the most jobs per minute.

The system throughput for varying user load levels is presented at right ⇒

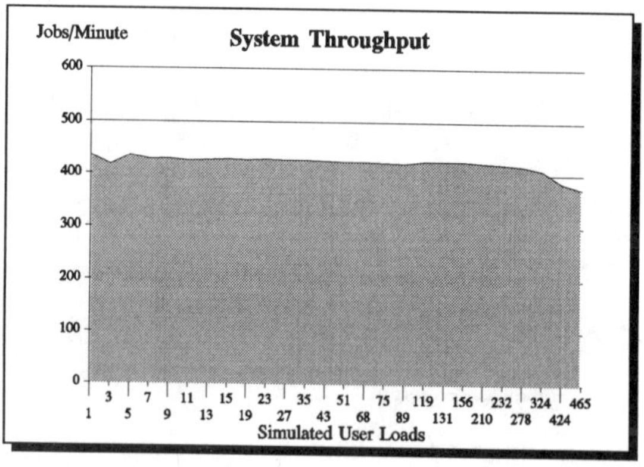

Maximum Throughput

435.7 Jobs/Minute

AIM Performance Report II

A UNIX Performance Summary Based on the AIM Benchmarks

Hewlett-Packard 9000 Model G50

Price	*Cpu Type*	*Clock Rate*	*Ext. Cpu Cache*	*Floating Point*	*RAM*
$77,745	PA-RISC 7100	96 MHz	256K data, 256K inst	Integrated	256 MB

Disks	*Disk Controllers*	*I/O Buffers*	*O/S*	*File System*	*Compiler*
2 GB, 11ms (2) 1.0 GB, 10.5ms (7)	Internal SE SCSI HP-PB FW SCSI	150 MB	HP-UX 9.04	BSD	HP C X.10.03

AIM Performance Rating

91.4 AIMs

The **AIM Performance Rating** reflects the peak performance of this system measured in AIM Multiuser Performance Units. A VAX 11/780 typically rates 1 AIM. Performance Ratings of a wide range of UNIX systems can be compared using available AIM Performance Reports.

Maximum User Load

820 User Loads

The **Maximum User Load** indicates the multitasking user load where the system's performance could become unacceptable, i.e. less than 1 job/minute/user load.

Utilities Index

Utilities Missing

Miles per Hour (MPH) is the number of *Milestone* User Loads that this system completes per hour. Milestone exercises selected UNIX utilities as foreground and background tasks at moderate user loads.

System Throughput is the total amount of work the system processes, measured in jobs per minute.

Maximum Throughput is the point at which the system is able to process the most jobs per minute.

The system throughput for varying user load levels is presented at right ⇒

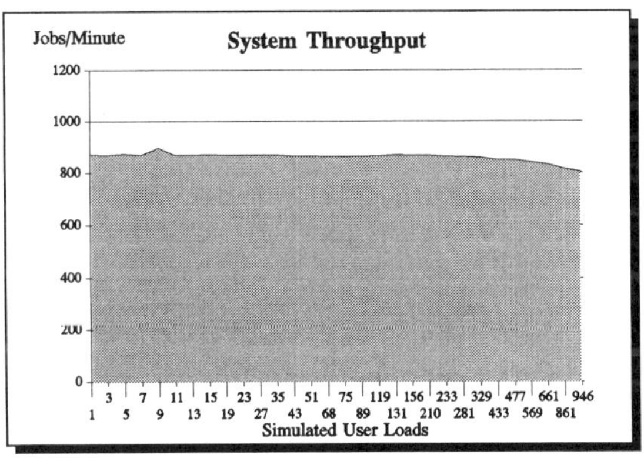

Maximum Throughput

895.3 Jobs/Minute

AIM Performance Report II

A UNIX Performance Summary Based on the AIM Benchmarks

Hewlett-Packard 9000 Model T500

Price	*Cpu Type*	*Clock Rate*	*Ext. Cpu Cache*	*Floating Point*	*RAM*
$218,212	PA-RISC 7100	90 MHz	1 MB data 1 MB inst	Integrated	256 MB

Disks	*Disk Controllers*	*I/O Buffers*	*O/S*	*File System*	*Compiler*
1.36 GB, 13.5ms (2) 1.0 GB, 10.5ms (10)	HP-FL HP-PB FW SCSI	150 MB	HP-UX 9.04	BSD	HP C X.10.03

AIM Performance Rating

88.7 AIMs

The **AIM Performance Rating** reflects the peak performance of this system measured in AIM Multiuser Performance Units. A VAX 11/780 typically rates 1 AIM. Performance Ratings of a wide range of UNIX systems can be compared using available AIM Performance Reports.

Maximum User Load

775 User Loads

The **Maximum User Load** indicates the multitasking user load where the system's performance could become unacceptable, i.e. less than 1 job/minute/user load.

Utilities Index

Utilities Missing

Miles per Hour (MPH) is the number of *Milestone* User Loads that this system completes per hour. Milestone exercises selected UNIX utilities as foreground and background tasks at moderate user loads.

System Throughput is the total amount of work the system processes, measured in jobs per minute.

Maximum Throughput is the point at which the system is able to process the most jobs per minute.

The system throughput for varying user load levels is presented at right ⇒

Maximum Throughput

869.3 Jobs/Minute

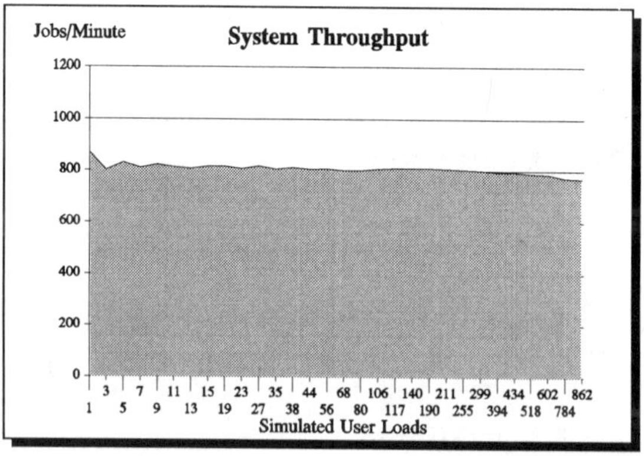

AIM Performance Report II

A UNIX Performance Summary Based on the AIM Benchmarks

IBM RISC System/6000 POWERserver 580H

Price	*Cpu Type*	*Clock Rate*	*Ext. Cpu Cache*	*Floating Point*	*RAM*
$77,754	IBM POWER2	55 MHz	256K data, 32K inst	Integrated	192 MB

Disks	*Disk Controllers*	*I/O Buffers*	*O/S*	*File System*	*Compiler*
IBM 2.0 GB, 11.5ms	SCSI	Dynamic	AIX Version 3.2.5	AIX/JFS	xlc v1.3

AIM Performance Rating

63.3 AIMs

The **AIM Performance Rating** reflects the peak performance of this system measured in AIM Multiuser Performance Units. A VAX 11/780 typically rates 1 AIM. Performance Ratings of a wide range of UNIX systems can be compared using available AIM Performance Reports.

Maximum User Load

582 User Loads

The **Maximum User Load** indicates the multitasking user load where the system's performance could become unacceptable, i.e. less than 1 job/minute/user load.

Utilities Index

Utilities Missing

Miles per Hour (MPH) is the number of *Milestone* User Loads that this system completes per hour. Milestone exercises selected UNIX utilities as foreground and background tasks at moderate user loads.

System Throughput is the total amount of work the system processes, measured in jobs per minute.

Maximum Throughput is the point at which the system is able to process the most jobs per minute.

The system throughput for varying user load levels is presented at right ⇒

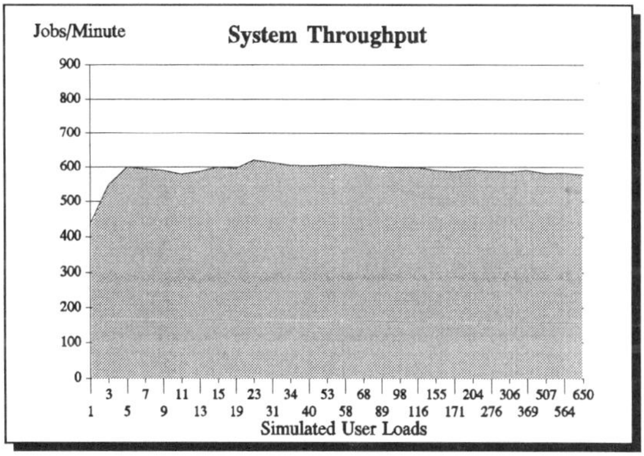

Maximum Throughput

620.5 Jobs/Minute

AIM Performance Report II

A UNIX Performance Summary Based on the AIM Benchmarks

IBM RISC System/6000 POWERserver 590

Price	Cpu Type	Clock Rate	Ext. Cpu Cache	Floating Point	RAM
$97,354	IBM POWER2	66.6 MHz	32K inst, 256K data	Integrated	128 MB

Disks	Disk Controllers	I/O Buffers	O/S	File System	Compiler
IBM 2.0 GB, 11.5ms (4)	SCSI	Dynamic	AIX Version 3.2.5 Beta	AIX/JFS	xlc v1.3

AIM Performance Rating

103.6 AIMs

The **AIM Performance Rating** reflects the peak performance of this system measured in AIM Multiuser Performance Units. A VAX 11/780 typically rates 1 AIM. Performance Ratings of a wide range of UNIX systems can be compared using available AIM Performance Reports.

Maximum User Load

803 User Loads

The **Maximum User Load** indicates the multitasking user load where the system's performance could become unacceptable, i.e. less than 1 job/minute/user load.

Utilities Index

Utilities Missing

Miles per Hour (MPH) is the number of *Milestone* User Loads that this system completes per hour. Milestone exercises selected UNIX utilities as foreground and background tasks at moderate user loads.

System Throughput is the total amount of work the system processes, measured in jobs per minute.

Maximum Throughput is the point at which the system is able to process the most jobs per minute.

The system throughput for varying user load levels is presented at right ⇒

Maximum Throughput

1015 Jobs/Minute

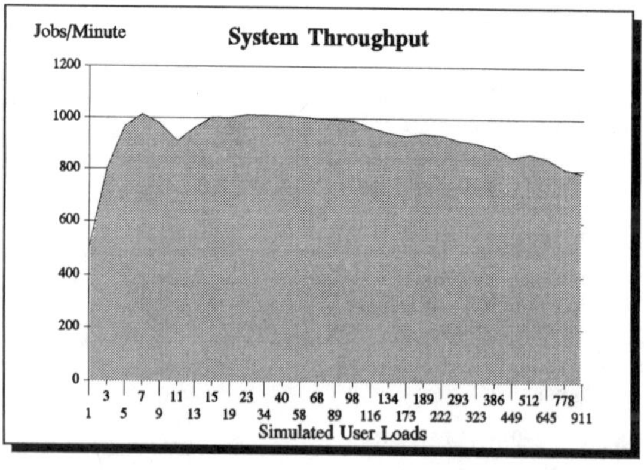

AIM Performance Report II

A UNIX Performance Summary Based on the AIM Benchmarks

IBM RISC System/6000 POWERstation 250

Price	*Cpu Type*	*Clock Rate*	*Ext. Cpu Cache*	*Floating Point*	*RAM*
$15,219	POWER PC 601	66.67 MHz	32K	Integrated	96 MB

Disks	*Disk Controllers*	*I/O Buffers*	*O/S*	*File System*	*Compiler*
IBM 1.0 GB, 11.5ms	SCSI	Dynamic	AIX Version 3.2.5	AIX/JFS	xlc v1.3

AIM Performance Rating

50.5 AIMs

The **AIM Performance Rating** reflects the peak performance of this system measured in AIM Multiuser Performance Units. A VAX 11/780 typically rates 1 AIM. Performance Ratings of a wide range of UNIX systems can be compared using available AIM Performance Reports.

Maximum User Load

421 User Loads

The **Maximum User Load** indicates the multitasking user load where the system's performance could become unacceptable, i.e. less than 1 job/minute/user load.

Utilities Index

Utilities Missing

Miles per Hour (MPH) is the number of Milestone User Loads that this system completes per hour. Milestone exercises selected UNIX utilities as foreground and background tasks at moderate user loads.

System Throughput is the total amount of work the system processes, measured in jobs per minute.

Maximum Throughput is the point at which the system is able to process the most jobs per minute.

The system throughput for varying user load levels is presented at right ⇒

Maximum Throughput

495.3 Jobs/Minute

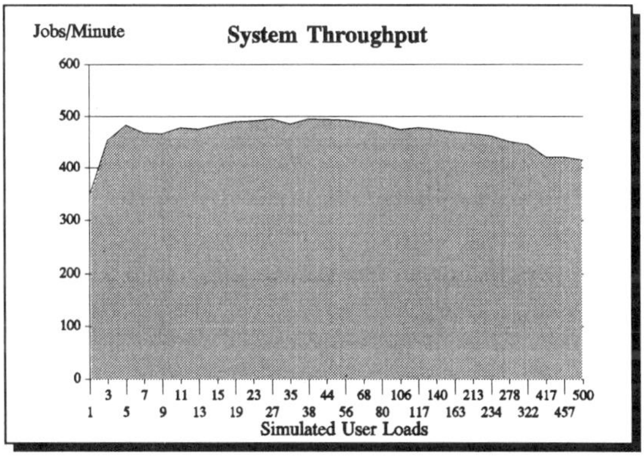

AIM Performance Report II

A UNIX Performance Summary Based on the AIM Benchmarks

ICL DRS 6000 Level 380

Price	*Cpu Type*	*Clock Rate*	*Ext. Cpu Cache*	*Floating Point*	*RAM*
$30,055	SuperSPARC	50 MHz	16K data, 20K inst 1st 1 MB 2nd lvl	Integrated	96 MB
Disks	***Disk Controllers***	***I/O Buffers***	***O/S***	***File System***	***Compiler***
1.2 GB, 10.5ms (2)	Integrated SCSI??	Dynamic	SVR 4.2 v711i2	VxFS	GNU C v2.3.3

AIM Performance Rating

71 AIMs

The **AIM Performance Rating** reflects the peak performance of this system measured in AIM Multiuser Performance Units. A VAX 11/780 typically rates 1 AIM. Performance Ratings of a wide range of UNIX systems can be compared using available AIM Performance Reports.

Maximum User Load

642 User Loads

The **Maximum User Load** indicates the multitasking user load where the system's performance could become unacceptable, i.e. less than 1 job/minute/user load.

Utilities Index

Utilities Missing

Miles per Hour (MPH) is the number of *Milestone* User Loads that this system completes per hour. Milestone exercises selected UNIX utilities as foreground and background tasks at moderate user loads.

System Throughput is the total amount of work the system processes, measured in jobs per minute.

Maximum Throughput is the point at which the system is able to process the most jobs per minute.

The system throughput for varying user load levels is presented at right ⇒

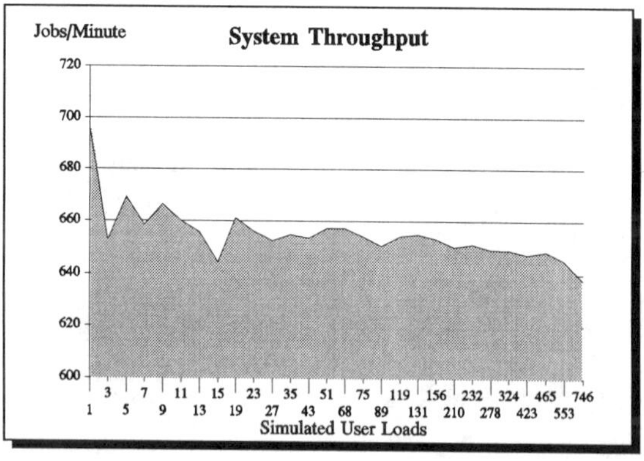

Maximum Throughput

696 Jobs/Minute

AIM Performance Report II

A UNIX Performance Summary Based on the AIM Benchmarks

ICL DRS 6000 Level 382

Price	Cpu Type	Clock Rate	Ext. Cpu Cache	Floating Point	RAM
$46,710	SuperSPARC (2)	50 MHz	16K data, 20K inst 1st 1 MB 2nd lvl	Integrated	128 MB
Disks	**Disk Controllers**	**I/O Buffers**	**O/S**	**File System**	**Compiler**
1.2 GB, 10.5ms (2)	Integrated SCSI??	Dynamic	SVR 4.2 v7l1i2	VxFS	GNU C v2.3.3

AIM Performance Rating

111 AIMs

The **AIM Performance Rating** reflects the peak performance of this system measured in AIM Multiuser Performance Units. A VAX 11/780 typically rates 1 AIM. Performance Ratings of a wide range of UNIX systems can be compared using available AIM Performance Reports.

Maximum User Load

1025 User Loads

The **Maximum User Load** indicates the multitasking user load where the system's performance could become unacceptable, i.e. less than 1 job/minute/user load.

Utilities Index

Utilities Missing

Miles per Hour (MPH) is the number of *Milestone* User Loads that this system completes per hour. Milestone exercises selected UNIX utilities as foreground and background tasks at moderate user loads.

System Throughput is the total amount of work the system processes, measured in jobs per minute.

Maximum Throughput is the point at which the system is able to process the most jobs per minute.

The system throughput for varying user load levels is presented at right ⇒

Maximum Throughput

1087.5 Jobs/Minute

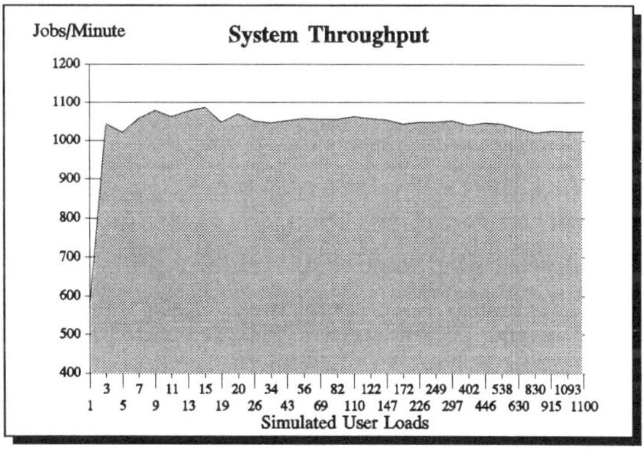

AIM Performance Report II

A UNIX Performance Summary Based on the AIM Benchmarks

NetFRAME NF250CS

Price	*Cpu Type*	*Clock Rate*	*Ext. Cpu Cache*	*Floating Point*	*RAM*
$59,908	Pentium	66 MHz	256K	Integrated	128 MB

Disks	*Disk Controllers*	*I/O Buffers*	*O/S*	*File System*	*Compiler*
550 MB, 11ms (3) 1.05 GB, 11ms	SCSI-II	Dynamic	UnixWare V1.0	VXFS	UnixWare V1.0 SDK (Rev. A)

AIM Performance Rating

71 AIMs

The **AIM Performance Rating** reflects the peak performance of this system measured in AIM Multiuser Performance Units. A VAX 11/780 typically rates 1 AIM. Performance Ratings of a wide range of UNIX systems can be compared using available AIM Performance Reports.

Maximum User Load

522 User Loads

The **Maximum User Load** indicates the multitasking user load where the system's performance could become unacceptable, i.e. less than 1 job/minute/user load.

Utilities Index

Utilities Missing

Miles per Hour (MPH) is the number of *Milestone* User Loads that this system completes per hour. Milestone exercises selected UNIX utilities as foreground and background tasks at moderate user loads.

System Throughput is the total amount of work the system processes, measured in jobs per minute.

Maximum Throughput is the point at which the system is able to process the most jobs per minute.

The system throughput for varying user load levels is presented at right ⇒

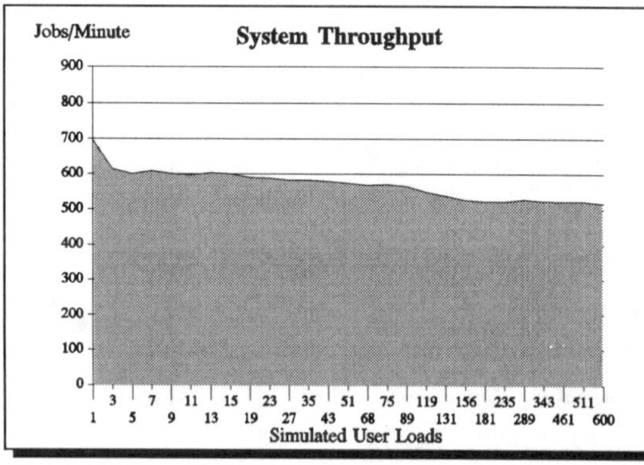

Maximum Throughput

696 Jobs/Minute

AIM Performance Report II

A UNIX Performance Summary Based on the AIM Benchmarks

Olivetti LSX 5025 Enhanced

Price	*Cpu Type*	*Clock Rate*	*Ext. Cpu Cache*	*Floating Point*	*RAM*
$11,349	80486DX2	33/66 MHz	128K	Integrated	48 MB

Disks	*Disk Controllers*	*I/O Buffers*	*O/S*	*File System*	*Compiler*
340 MB, 14ms	Dual Channel SCSI	Dynamic	SVR4.0 v2.2.1	UFS	AT&T C

AIM Performance Rating

28.9 AIMs

The **AIM Performance Rating** reflects the peak performance of this system measured in AIM Multiuser Performance Units. A VAX 11/780 typically rates 1 AIM. Performance Ratings of a wide range of UNIX systems can be compared using available AIM Performance Reports.

Maximum User Load

275 User Loads

The **Maximum User Load** indicates the multitasking user load where the system's performance could become unacceptable, i.e. less than 1 job/minute/user load.

Utilities Index

70.1 MPH

Miles per Hour (MPH) is the number of *Milestone* User Loads that this system completes per hour. Milestone exercises selected UNIX utilities as foreground and background tasks at moderate user loads.

System Throughput is the total amount of work the system processes, measured in jobs per minute.

Maximum Throughput is the point at which the system is able to process the most jobs per minute.

The system throughput for varying user load levels is presented at right ⇒

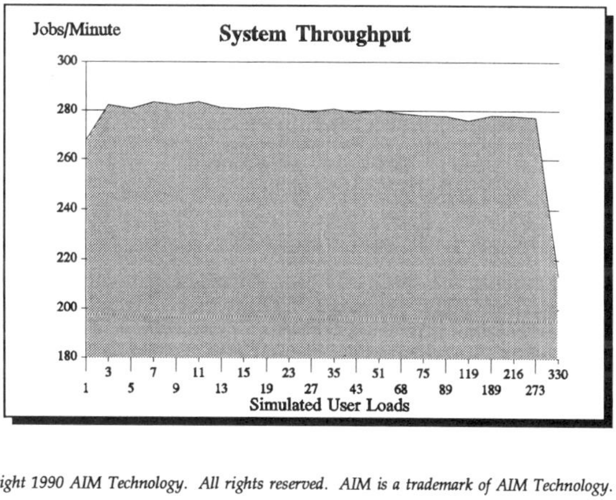

Maximum Throughput

283.6 Jobs/Minute

AIM Performance Report II

A UNIX Performance Summary Based on the AIM Benchmarks

Olivetti LSX 5040 Enhanced

Price	Cpu Type	Clock Rate	Ext. Cpu Cache	Floating Point	RAM
$23,079	80486DX2	33/66 MHz	1 MB	Integrated	48 MB

Disks	Disk Controllers	I/O Buffers	O/S	File System	Compiler
525 MB, 14ms	ESC2 SCSI	Dynamic	SVR4.0 v2.2.1	UFS	AT&T C

AIM Performance Rating

36.2 AIMs

The **AIM Performance Rating** reflects the peak performance of this system measured in AIM Multiuser Performance Units. A VAX 11/780 typically rates 1 AIM. Performance Ratings of a wide range of UNIX systems can be compared using available AIM Performance Reports.

Maximum User Load

332 User Loads

The **Maximum User Load** indicates the multitasking user load where the system's performance could become unacceptable, i.e. less than 1 job/minute/user load.

Utilities Index

71.2 MPH

Miles per Hour (MPH) is the number of *Milestone* User Loads that this system completes per hour. Milestone exercises selected UNIX utilities as foreground and background tasks at moderate user loads.

System Throughput is the total amount of work the system processes, measured in jobs per minute.

Maximum Throughput is the point at which the system is able to process the most jobs per minute.

The system throughput for varying user load levels is presented at right ⇒

Maximum Throughput

355.1 Jobs/Minute

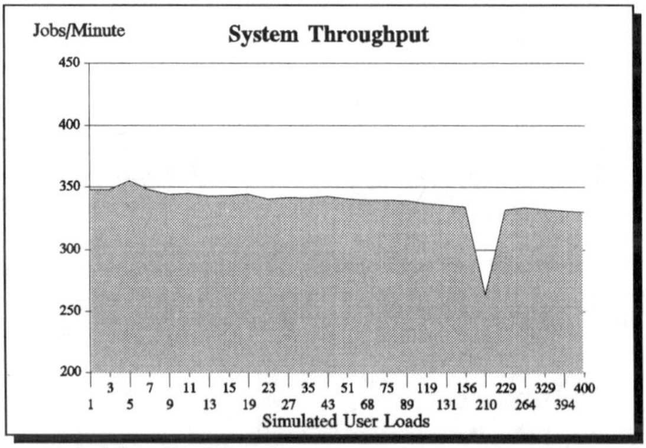

AIM Performance Report II

A UNIX Performance Summary Based on the AIM Benchmarks

Olivetti LSX 5040/2 Enhanced

Price	Cpu Type	Clock Rate	Ext. Cpu Cache	Floating Point	RAM
$31,174	80486DX2 (2)	33/66 MHz	1 MB	Integrated	96 MB

Disks	Disk Controllers	I/O Buffers	O/S	File System	Compiler
525 MB, 14ms (2)	ESC2 SCSI	Dynamic	SVR4.0 v2.2.1 MP	UFS	AT&T C

AIM Performance Rating

60.8 AIMs

The **AIM Performance Rating** reflects the peak performance of this system measured in AIM Multiuser Performance Units. A VAX 11/780 typically rates 1 AIM. Performance Ratings of a wide range of UNIX systems can be compared using available AIM Performance Reports.

Maximum User Load

559 User Loads

The **Maximum User Load** indicates the multitasking user load where the system's performance could become unacceptable, i.e. less than 1 job/minute/user load.

Utilities Index

147.9 MPH

Miles per Hour (MPH) is the number of Milestone User Loads that this system completes per hour. Milestone exercises selected UNIX utilities as foreground and background tasks at moderate user loads.

System Throughput is the total amount of work the system processes, measured in jobs per minute.

Maximum Throughput is the point at which the system is able to process the most jobs per minute.

The system throughput for varying user load levels is presented at right ⇒

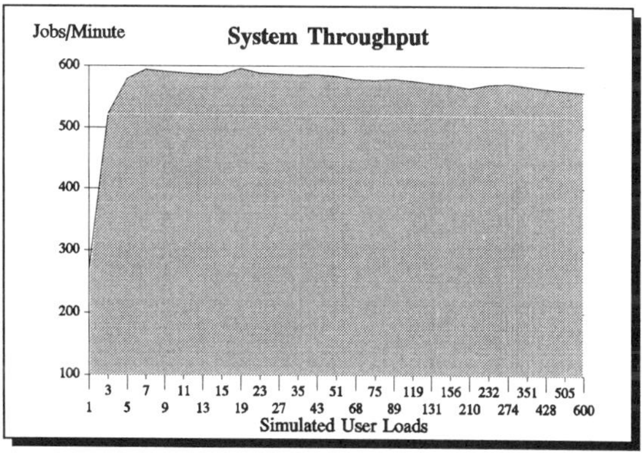

Maximum Throughput

595.7 Jobs/Minute

AIM Performance Report II

A UNIX Performance Summary Based on the AIM Benchmarks

Olivetti LSX 5040/3 Enhanced

Price	Cpu Type	Clock Rate	Ext. Cpu Cache	Floating Point	RAM
$37,854	80486DX2 (3)	33/66 MHz	1 MB	Integrated	128 MB

Disks	Disk Controllers	I/O Buffers	O/S	File System	Compiler
525 MB, 14ms (2)	ESC2 SCSI	Dynamic	SVR4.0 v2.2.1 MP	UFS	AT&T C

AIM Performance Rating

88.8 AIMs

The **AIM Performance Rating** reflects the peak performance of this system measured in AIM Multiuser Performance Units. A VAX 11/780 typically rates 1 AIM. Performance Ratings of a wide range of UNIX systems can be compared using available AIM Performance Reports.

Maximum User Load

771 User Loads

The **Maximum User Load** indicates the multitasking user load where the system's performance could become unacceptable, i.e. less than 1 job/minute/user load.

Utilities Index

167.7 MPH

Miles per Hour (MPH) is the number of *Milestone* User Loads that this system completes per hour. Milestone exercises selected UNIX utilities as foreground and background tasks at moderate user loads.

System Throughput is the total amount of work the system processes, measured in jobs per minute.

Maximum Throughput is the point at which the system is able to process the most jobs per minute.

The system throughput for varying user load levels is presented at right ⇒

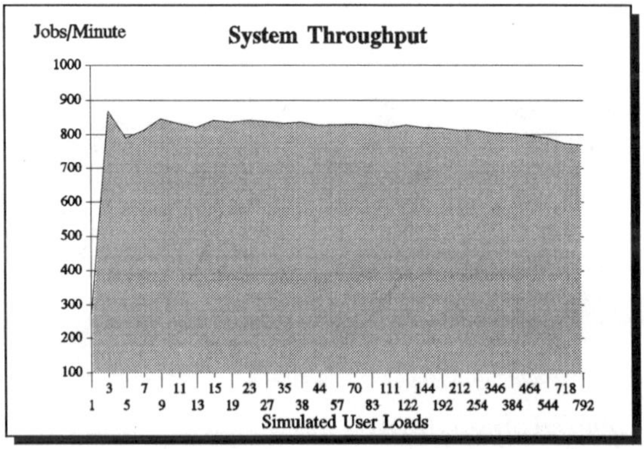

Maximum Throughput

870 Jobs/Minute

AIM Performance Report II

A UNIX Performance Summary Based on the AIM Benchmarks

Olivetti LSX 5040/4 Enhanced

Price	*Cpu Type*	*Clock Rate*	*Ext. Cpu Cache*	*Floating Point*	*RAM*
$42,396	80486DX2 (4)	33/66 MHz	1MB	Integrated	128 MB
Disks	*Disk Controllers*	*I/O Buffers*	*O/S*	*File System*	*Compiler*
525 MB, 14ms (4)	ESC2 SCSI	Dynamic	SVR4.0 v2.2.1 MP	UFS	AT&T C

AIM Performance Rating

110.6 AIMs

The **AIM Performance Rating** reflects the peak performance of this system measured in AIM Multiuser Performance Units. A VAX 11/780 typically rates 1 AIM. Performance Ratings of a wide range of UNIX systems can be compared using available AIM Performance Reports.

Maximum User Load

905 User Loads

The **Maximum User Load** indicates the multitasking user load where the system's performance could become unacceptable, i.e. less than 1 job/minute/user load.

Utilities Index

211.1 MPH

Miles per Hour (MPH) is the number of *Milestone* User Loads that this system completes per hour. Milestone exercises selected UNIX utilities as foreground and background tasks at moderate user loads.

System Throughput is the total amount of work the system processes, measured in jobs per minute.

Maximum Throughput is the point at which the system is able to process the most jobs per minute.

The system throughput for varying user load levels is presented at right ⇒

Maximum Throughput

1083.9 Jobs/Minute

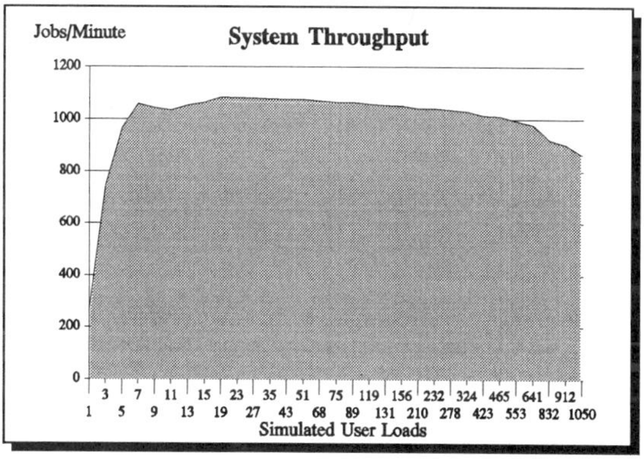

AIM Performance Report II

A UNIX Performance Summary Based on the AIM Benchmarks

Silicon Graphics CHALLENGE L

Price	*Cpu Type*	*Clock Rate*	*Ext. Cpu Cache*	*Floating Point*	*RAM*
$139,100	MIPS R4400 (2)	75/150 MHz	16K data, 16K inst-on-chip, 1MB 2nd lvl	MIPS R4010 (2)	256 MB
Disks	*Disk Controllers*	*I/O Buffers*	*O/S*	*File System*	*Compiler*
2.0 GB, 9.4ms (4)	Integrated SCSI-II	Dynamic	IRIX 5.1	EFS	ANSI C 3.17

AIM Performance Rating

152.5 AIMs

The **AIM Performance Rating** reflects the peak performance of this system measured in AIM Multiuser Performance Units. A VAX 11/780 typically rates 1 AIM. Performance Ratings of a wide range of UNIX systems can be compared using available AIM Performance Reports.

Maximum User Load

1173 User Loads

The **Maximum User Load** indicates the multitasking user load where the system's performance could become unacceptable, i.e. less than 1 job/minute/user load.

Utilities Index

Utilities Missing

Miles per Hour (MPH) is the number of *Milestone* User Loads that this system completes per hour. Milestone exercises selected UNIX utilities as foreground and background tasks at moderate user loads.

System Throughput is the total amount of work the system processes, measured in jobs per minute.

Maximum Throughput is the point at which the system is able to process the most jobs per minute.

The system throughput for varying user load levels is presented at right ⇒

Maximum Throughput

1494.5 Jobs/Minute

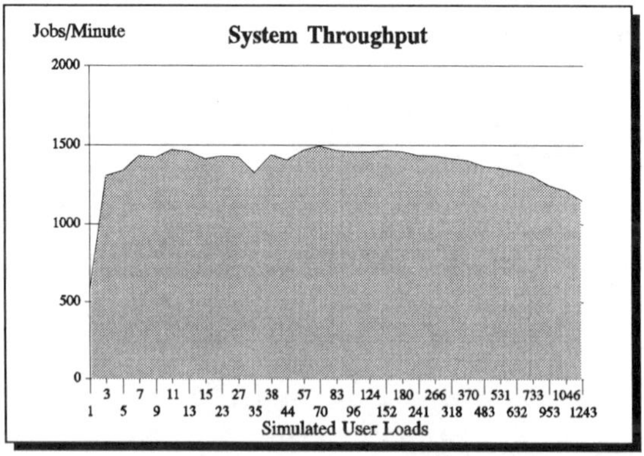

AIM Performance Report II

A UNIX Performance Summary Based on the AIM Benchmarks

Silicon Graphics CHALLENGE L

Price	*Cpu Type*	*Clock Rate*	*Ext. Cpu Cache*	*Floating Point*	*RAM*
$196,900	MIPS R4400 (4)	75/150 MHz	16K data, 16K inst-on-chip, 1MB 2nd lvl	R4010 (4)	256 MB
Disks	***Disk Controllers***	***I/O Buffers***	***O/S***	***File System***	***Compiler***
2.0 GB, 9.4ms (6)	Integrated SCSI-II	Dynamic	IRIX 5.1	EFS	ANSI C 3.17

AIM Performance Rating

245.8 AIMs

The **AIM Performance Rating** reflects the peak performance of this system measured in AIM Multiuser Performance Units. A VAX 11/780 typically rates 1 AIM. Performance Ratings of a wide range of UNIX systems can be compared using available AIM Performance Reports.

Maximum User Load

1739 User Loads

The **Maximum User Load** indicates the multitasking user load where the system's performance could become unacceptable, i.e. less than 1 job/minute/user load.

Utilities Index

Utilities Missing

Miles per Hour (MPH) is the number of *Milestone* User Loads that this system completes per hour. Milestone exercises selected UNIX utilities as foreground and background tasks at moderate user loads.

System Throughput is the total amount of work the system processes, measured in jobs per minute.

Maximum Throughput is the point at which the system is able to process the most jobs per minute.

The system throughput for varying user load levels is presented at right ⇒

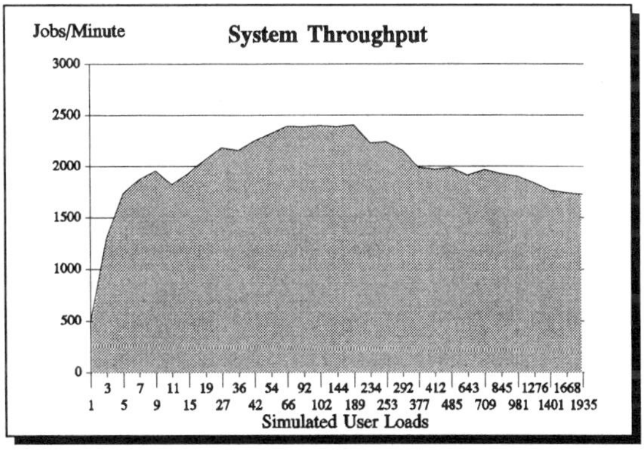

Maximum Throughput

2409.2 Jobs/Minute

AIM Performance Report II

A UNIX Performance Summary Based on the AIM Benchmarks

Silicon Graphics Challenge M/Indigo 2

Price	*Cpu Type*	*Clock Rate*	*Ext. Cpu Cache*	*Floating Point*	*RAM*
$30,900	MIPS R4400SC	75/150 MHz	1 MB 2nd lvl	Integrated	96 MB
Disks	*Disk Controllers*	*I/O Buffers*	*O/S*	*File System*	*Compiler*
1 GB, 12ms	Integrated SCSI-2	Dynamic	IRIX 5.1	EFS	ANSI C 3.17

AIM Performance Rating

113.3 AIMs

The **AIM Performance Rating** reflects the peak performance of this system measured in AIM Multiuser Performance Units. A VAX 11/780 typically rates 1 AIM. Performance Ratings of a wide range of UNIX systems can be compared using available AIM Performance Reports.

Maximum User Load

798 User Loads

The **Maximum User Load** indicates the multitasking user load where the system's performance could become unacceptable, i.e. less than 1 job/minute/user load.

Utilities Index

Utilities Missing

Miles per Hour (MPH) is the number of *Milestone* User Loads that this system completes per hour. Milestone exercises selected UNIX utilities as foreground and background tasks at moderate user loads.

System Throughput is the total amount of work the system processes, measured in jobs per minute.

Maximum Throughput is the point at which the system is able to process the most jobs per minute.

The system throughput for varying user load levels is presented at right ⇒

Maximum Throughput

1110.6 Jobs/Minute

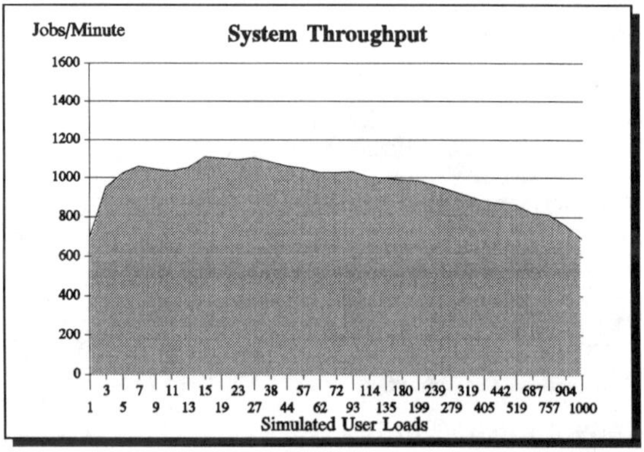

AIM Performance Report II

A UNIX Performance Summary Based on the AIM Benchmarks

Silicon Graphics Indy R4000SC

Price	*Cpu Type*	*Clock Rate*	*Ext. Cpu Cache*	*Floating Point*	*RAM*
$14,495	MIPS R4000SC	50/100 MHz	1 MB	Integrated	48 MB

Disks	*Disk Controllers*	*I/O Buffers*	*O/S*	*File System*	*Compiler*
535 MB, 12ms	Integrated SCSI-II	Dynamic	IRIX 5.1	EFS	ANSI C 3.17

AIM Performance Rating

71 AIMs

The **AIM Performance Rating** reflects the peak performance of this system measured in AIM Multiuser Performance Units. A VAX 11/780 typically rates 1 AIM. Performance Ratings of a wide range of UNIX systems can be compared using available AIM Performance Reports.

Maximum User Load

442 User Loads

The **Maximum User Load** indicates the multitasking user load where the system's performance could become unacceptable, i.e. less than 1 job/minute/user load.

Utilities Index

Utilities Missing

Miles per Hour (MPH) is the number of *Milestone* User Loads that this system completes per hour. Milestone exercises selected UNIX utilities as foreground and background tasks at moderate user loads.

System Throughput is the total amount of work the system processes, measured in jobs per minute.

Maximum Throughput is the point at which the system is able to process the most jobs per minute.

The system throughput for varying user load levels is presented at right ⇒

Maximum Throughput

696 Jobs/Minute

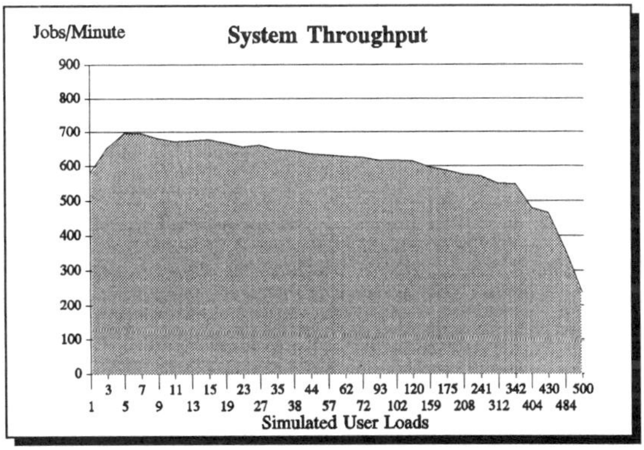

AIM Performance Report II

A UNIX Performance Summary Based on the AIM Benchmarks

Sun SPARCcenter 1000

Price	Cpu Type	Clock Rate	Ext. Cpu Cache	Floating Point	RAM
$80,500	SuperSPARC (4)	50 MHz	36K/cpu 1st 1 MB/cpu 2nd lvl	Integrated	128 MB

Disks	Disk Controllers	I/O Buffers	O/S	File System	Compiler
535 MB, 12ms (6)	Integrated FSBE (2)	Dynamic +4 MB PrestoServe	Solaris 2.3	UFS	SC 2.0.1

AIM Performance Rating

138.2 AIMs

The **AIM Performance Rating** reflects the peak performance of this system measured in AIM Multiuser Performance Units. A VAX 11/780 typically rates 1 AIM. Performance Ratings of a wide range of UNIX systems can be compared using available AIM Performance Reports.

Maximum User Load

1149 User Loads

The **Maximum User Load** indicates the multitasking user load where the system's performance could become unacceptable, i.e. less than 1 job/minute/user load.

Utilities Index

118.6 MPH

Miles per Hour (MPH) is the number of *Milestone* User Loads that this system completes per hour. Milestone exercises selected UNIX utilities as foreground and background tasks at moderate user loads.

System Throughput is the total amount of work the system processes, measured in jobs per minute.

Maximum Throughput is the point at which the system is able to process the most jobs per minute.

The system throughput for varying user load levels is presented at right ⇒

Maximum Throughput

1354.8 Jobs/Minute

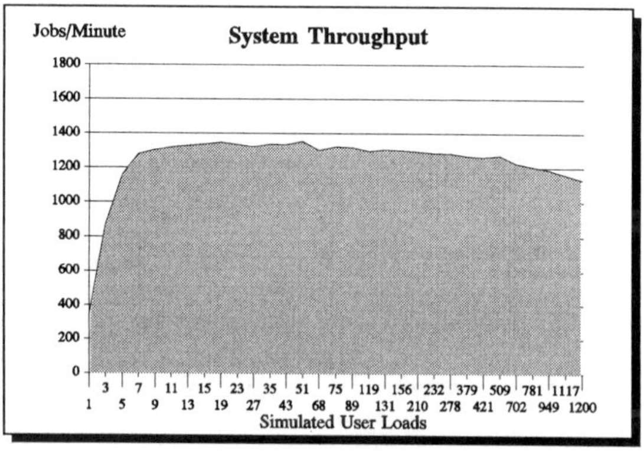

AIM Performance Report II

A UNIX Performance Summary Based on the AIM Benchmarks

Sun SPARCcenter 2000

Price	*Cpu Type*	*Clock Rate*	*Ext. Cpu Cache*	*Floating Point*	*RAM*
$293,735	SuperSPARC (8)	50 MHz	36K per cpu 1st 2 MB per cpu 2nd lvl	Integrated	384 MB
Disks	***Disk Controllers***	***I/O Buffers***	***O/S***	***File System***	***Compiler***
2.1 GB, 11ms (12)	DSCSI (4)	Dynamic +8 MB PrestoServe	Solaris 2.3	UFS	SC 2.0.1

AIM Performance Rating

259.5 AIMs

The **AIM Performance Rating** reflects the peak performance of this system measured in AIM Multiuser Performance Units. A VAX 11/780 typically rates 1 AIM. Performance Ratings of a wide range of UNIX systems can be compared using available AIM Performance Reports.

Maximum User Load

1969 User Loads

The **Maximum User Load** indicates the multitasking user load where the system's performance could become unacceptable, i.e. less than 1 job/minute/user load.

Utilities Index

202.2 MPH

Miles per Hour (MPH) is the number of *Milestone* User Loads that this system completes per hour. Milestone exercises selected UNIX utilities as foreground and background tasks at moderate user loads.

System Throughput is the total amount of work the system processes, measured in jobs per minute.

Maximum Throughput is the point at which the system is able to process the most jobs per minute.

The system throughput for varying user load levels is presented at right ⇒

Maximum Throughput

2543.1 Jobs/Minute

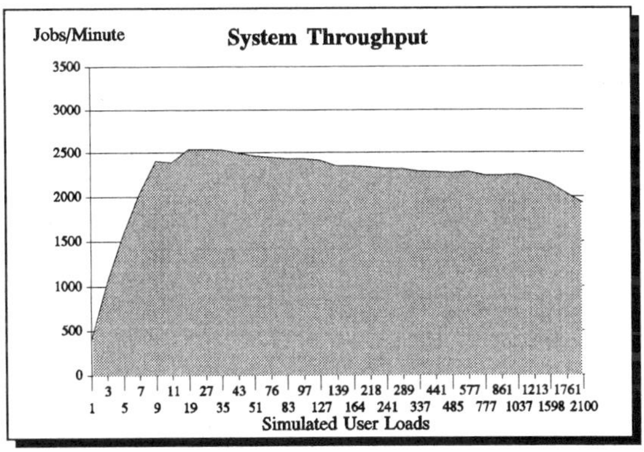

System Performance: Buyer's Guide

	AcerAltos 700	AcerAltos 7000	AcerAltos 7000	AcerAltos 17000
AIM Performance Rating	25.9	26.9	38.8	50.7
Maximum User Load	141	225	290	343
Price	$4,800	$7,006	$8,106	$17,025
CPU Type	486DX2-66	486DX2	Pentium	Pentium
Clock Rate	66/33 MHz	33/66 MHz	33 MHz	60 MHz
External CPU Cache	128K 2nd lvl	256K	512K 2nd lvl	256K
Floating Point	Integrated	Integrated	Integrated	Integrated
RAM	16 MB	64 MB	64 MB	64 MB
Disks	520 MB, 12ms (3)	520 MB, 12ms (3)	520 MB, 12ms (3)	520 MB, 12ms (4)
Disk Controllers	Adaptec 6360 SCSI	Adaptec 7770 SCSI II	Adaptec 7770 SCSI II	SCA II SCSI
I/O Buffers	6960 KB	32768 KB	32768 KB	32 MB
O/S	Altos/SCO UNIX 4.1b	Altos/SCO UNIX 4.1b	Altos/SCO UNIX 4.1b	Altos/SCO UNIX 4.1b
File System	EAFS	EAFS	EAFS	EAFS
Compiler	Metaware High C v2.32	Metaware High C v2.32	SCO C Compiler v1.1.4	SCO C Compiler v1.1.4

	Altos System 15000	Altos System 15000	Altos System 15000	Apple Workgroup Server 95
AIM Performance Rating	27.8	51.8	86.4	22.2
Maximum User Load	255	379	565	137
Price	$27,808	$33,144	$42,968	$6,648
CPU Type	486DX	486DX (2)	486DX (4)	68040
Clock Rate	50 MHz	50 MHz	50 MHz	33 MHz
External CPU Cache	256K	256K per cpu	256K per cpu	256K
Floating Point	Integrated	Integrated	Integrated	Integrated
RAM	64 MB	64 MB	128 MB	32 MB
Disks	520 MB, 12ms (5)	520 MB, 12ms (8)	520 MB, 12ms (10)	500 MB, 12ms 230 MB, 16ms
Disk Controllers	Altos SCA SCSI-II	Altos SCA SCSI-II	Altos SCA SCSI-II (2)	NCR 53C96 SCSI
I/O Buffers	32 MB	32 MB	64 MB	Dynamic
O/S	Altos/SCO UNIX 4.0	Altos/SCO UNIX 4.0	Altos/SCO UNIX 4.0	A/UX 3.0.2
File System	AFS	AFS	AFS	BSD/UFS
Compiler	Metaware High C 2.32	Metaware High C 2.32	Metaware High C 2.32	c89 v1.1

System Performance: Buyer's Guide

	AST Manhattan SMP	AST Manhattan SMP	AST Manhattan SMP	Bull DPX/2 380 (2)
AIM Performance Rating	53.3	81.9	114.1	39.8
Maximum User Load	454	723	998	229
Price	$29,680	$49,334	$68,757	$59,898
CPU Type	Pentium	Pentium (2)	Pentium (4)	MC68040 (2)
Clock Rate	60 MHz	60 MHz	60 MHz	33 MHz
External CPU Cache	256KB 2nd lvl	256KB per cpu 2nd lvl	256KB per cpu 2nd lvl	256K per cpu
Floating Point	Integrated	Integrated	Integrated	Integrated
RAM	64 MB	128 MB	192 MB	96 MB
Disks	1 GB, 11ms (1) 500 MB, 10.5ms (1)	1 GB, 11 ms (1) 500 MB, 10.5ms (3)	1 GB, 11ms (1) 500 MB, 10.5ms (4)	Maxtor 500 MB, 12ms (3)
Disk Controllers	AST Empire SCSI-2 Array	AST Empire SCSI-2 Array (2)	AST Empire SCSI-2 Array (2)	Bull SCSI
I/O Buffers	25,000 KB	80,000 KB	90,000 KB	28 MB
O/S	SCO UNIX 3.2.4	SCO UNIX 3.2.4 w /MPX 3.0	SCO UNIX 3.2.4 w/MPX 3.0	B.O.S. 02.00.69
File System	EAFS	EAFS	EAFS	FFS
Compiler	SCO Optimizing C 1.1.4a	SCO Optimizing C 1.1.4a	SCO Optimizing C 1.1.4a	Green Hills 1.8.5

	Bull DPX/2 380 (4)	Bull DPX/20 140S	Bull DPX/20 440	Bull DPX/20 470
AIM Performance Rating	58.5	16.3	28.4	60.9
Maximum User Load	360	147	247	490
Price	$111,960	$13,600	$20,180	$42,300
CPU Type	MC68040 (4)	IBM POWER 3308	IBM POWER 3332	IBM POWER 6232
Clock Rate	33 MHz	33 MHz	33 MHz	62.5 MHz
External CPU Cache	256K per cpu	8K	32K data, 8K inst	32K data, 32K inst
Floating Point	Integrated	Integrated	Integrated	Integrated
RAM	224 MB	64 MB	64 MB	128 MB
Disks	Maxtor 500 MB, 12ms (4)	400 MB, 11.5ms (1) 320 MB, 12.5 (1)	400 MB, 11.5ms (2)	1 GB, 11.5ms (3)
Disk Controllers	Bull SCSI	Integrated SCSI	Integrated SCSI	IBM SCSI
I/O Buffers	28 MB	Dynamic	Dynamic	Dynamic
O/S	B.O.S. 02.00.69	BOSX v3.2	BOSX v3.2	BOSX v3.2.3
File System	FFS	AIX	AIX	AIX
Compiler	Green Hills 1.8.5	XlC v1.2	xlc v1.2	xlcv1.2

System Performance: Buyer's Guide

	Bull DPX/20 610	Bull DPX/20 620	Bull DPX/20 640	Bull DPX/20 660
AIM Performance Rating	22.4	29.7	47.7	62.1
Maximum User Load	198	251	428	518
Price	$32,180	$41,980	$54,950	$82,400
CPU Type	IBM POWER 2532	IBM POWER 3364	IBM POWER 5032	IBM POWER 6264
Clock Rate	25 MHz	33 MHz	50 MHz	62.5 MHz
External CPU Cache	32K data, 8K inst	64K data, 8K inst	32Kdata, 32K inst	64K data, 32K inst
Floating Point	Integrated	Integrated	Integrated	Integrated
RAM	64 MB	64 MB	128 MB	128 MB
Disks	400 MB, 11.5ms (2)	400 MB, 11.5ms (2)	1 GB, 11.5ms (3)	1GB, 11.5ms (4)
Disk Controllers	IBM SCSI	IBM SCSI	Integrated SCSI	Integrated SCSI
I/O Buffers	Dynamic	Dynamic	Dynamic	Dynamic
O/S	BOSX v3.2	BOSX v3.2	BOSX v3.2.3	BOSX v3.2.3
File System	AIX	AIX	AIX	AIX
Compiler	xlc v1.2	xlc v1.2	xlc v1.2.1	xld v1.2

	Bull DPX/20 810	Compaq ProLiant 1000 4/66 Model 2100A	Compaq ProLiant 1000 5/60 Model 2100A	Compaq ProLiant 2000 5/66 Model 2100A
AIM Performance Rating	49.9	29.1	44.4	104.4
Maximum User Load	454	284	406	998
Price	$97,100	$18,023	$19,464	$37,828
CPU Type	POWER 5064	486DX/2	Pentium	Pentium (2)
Clock Rate	50 MHz	33/66 MHz	60 MHz	66 MHz
External CPU Cache	64K data, 32K inst	256K	256K	256K
Floating Point	Integrated	Integrated	Integrated	Integrated
RAM	128 MB	64 MB	80 MB	192 MB
Disks	1.3 GB, 12ms (3)	1 GB, 10.5ms (3) Drive Array	1 GB, 10.5ms (3) Drive Array	1 GB, 10.5ms (3) Drive Array
Disk Controllers	IBM SCSI	Compaq SMART Array	Compaq SMART Array	Compaq SMART Array
I/O Buffers	Dynamic	32,768 KB	32,768 KB	65,536 KB
O/S	BOSX v3.2.1	SCO UNIX 3.2 v4.2	SCO UNIX 3.2 v4.2	SCO UNIX 3.2 v4.2 SCO MPX 3.0
File System	AIX	EAFS	EAFS	EAFS
Compiler	xlc v1.2	SCO Intel Reference	SCO Intel Reference	SCO Intel Reference

System Performance: Buyer's Guide

	Compaq ProSignia	Compaq SYSTEMPRO/ XL (486)	Compaq SYSTEMPRO/ XL (Pentium)	Control Data 4430 PC
AIM Performance Rating	30.2	54.4	103.1	40.7
Maximum User Load	222	529	976	340
Price	$12,017	$24,581	$40,796	$27,080
CPU Type	486DX2	486DX50 (2)	Pentium (2)	R4000
Clock Rate	66/33 MHz	50 MHz	66 MHz	50/100 MHz
External CPU Cache	256K	256K per cpu	256K per cpu	none
Floating Point	Integrated	Integrated	Integrated	Integrated
RAM	64 MB	112 MB	192 MB	64 MB
Disks	510 MB, 12ms (2)	550 MB, 10.5ms (4)	1 GB, 10.5ms (3)	535 MB, 12ms (1) 1.2 GB, 12ms (2)
Disk Controllers	COMPAQIDA-2 Disk Array	COMPAQ SMART Array	COMPAQ SMART Array	Integrated SCSI
I/O Buffers	30,400 KB	40,960 KB	65,536 KB	Dynamic
O/S	COMPAQ SCO UNIX 3.2 V4	SCO UNIX 3.2 V4 SCO MPX 3.0	SCO UNIX 3.2 V4 SCO MPX 3.0	EP/IX V.2.1.1
File System	EAFS	AFS	EAFS	FFS
Compiler	MetaWare High-C v2.3	SCO - Intel Reference	SCO Intel Reference	MIPS C v3.1

	Control Data 4440-102 InfoServer	Control Data 4460-103 InfoServer	Control Data 4680-312 InfoServer	Control Data 4680-312 InfoServer
AIM Performance Rating	59.2	56.6	76.4	78.1
Maximum User Load	478	473	734	725
Price	$40,520	$61,740	$124,363	$170,827
CPU Type	R4000	R4000	MIPS R6000A	MIPS R6000A
Clock Rate	50/100 MHz	50/100 MHz	80 MHz	80 MHz
External CPU Cache	8K d, 8K i/1MB 2nd	8K data, 8K inst	2 MB	2 MB
Floating Point	Integrated	Integrated	MIPS R6010	MIPS R6010
RAM	64 MB	64 MB	128 MB	128 MB
Disks	535 MB, 12ms (1) 1.2 GB, 12ms (3)	1 GB, 15ms (1) 1.2 GB, 9.8ms (3)	1 GB, 15.5ms (1) 663 MB, 15.5ms (2)	1 GB, 15.5ms 663 MB, 15.5ms (12)
Disk Controllers	Integrated SCSI	Integrated SCSI	CD 47002-3 SCSI	SCSI (4)
I/O Buffers	Dynamic	Dynamic	Dynamic	Dynamic
O/S	EP/IX V.2.1.1	EP/IX V.2.1.1	EP/IX v.1.4.3	EP/IX V1.4.3
File System	FFS	FFS	FFS	FFS
Compiler	MIPS C v3.1	MIPS C v3.1	MIPS 2.20	MIPS 2.20

System Performance: Buyer's Guide

	Control Data 4680-312	Control Data 4680-313 InfoServer (4 CPU)	Control Data 9130 (R4000)	Data General AViiON 4300
AIM Performance Rating	135.8	251.4	69.1	21.1
Maximum User Load	1285	2329	160	203
Price	$268,250	$282,965	$18,995	$19,359
CPU Type	MIPS R6000A (2)	MIPS R6000A (4)	R4000 SC	88100
Clock Rate	80 MHz	80 MHz	50/100 MHz	25 MHz
External CPU Cache	2 MB per cpu	8 MB	8K inst, 8K data, 1M 2nd	16K data, 16K inst
Floating Point	MIPS R6000A (2)	MIPS R6010	Integrated	Integrated
RAM	256 MB	384 MB	32 MB	48 MB
Disks	1 GB, 15.5ms (1) 663 MB, 15.5ms (21)	1 GB, 15.5ms (1) 663 MB, 15.5ms (11)	1.0 GB, 12ms	520 MB, 12ms
Disk Controllers	CD 47002-3 SCSI (6)	CD 47002-3 SCSI (2) CD47002-4 SCSI	Integrated SCSI	Integrated SCSI
I/O Buffers	Dynamic	Dynamic	Dynamic	Dynamic
O/S	EP/IX v.1.4.3	EP/IX v.1.4.3	IRIX 5.1.0.1	DG/UX 5.4.2
File System	FFS	FFS	EFS	DG/UX
Compiler	MIPS C 2.20	MIPS 2.20	MIPS C v3.17	gcc 2.2.2

	Data General AViiON 4320	Data General AViiON 4320	Data General AViiON 4605	Data General AViiON 4625
AIM Performance Rating	40.6	39.5	32.9	63.4
Maximum User Load	113	378	317	613
Price	$18,959	$33,759	$22,459	$36,559
CPU Type	88100 (2)	88100 (2)	88100	88100 (2)
Clock Rate	25 MHz	25 MHz	33 MHz	33 MHz
External CPU Cache	16K data, 16K inst per cpu	16K data, 16K inst	32K data, 64K inst	64K data, 32K inst per cpu
Floating Point	Integrated	Integrated	Integrated	Integrated
RAM	24 MB	80 MB	32 MB	64 MB
Disks	520 MB, 12ms	520 MB, 12ms (2)	520 MB, 12ms	520 MB, 12ms
Disk Controllers	Integrated SCSI	Integrated SCSI	Integrated SCSI	Integrated SCSI
I/O Buffers	Dynamic	Dynamic	Dynamic	Dynamic
O/S	DG/UX 5.4.1	DG/UX 5.4.2e01	DG/UX 5.4R2.01	DG/UX 5.4R2.01
File System	DG/UX	DG/UX	DG/UX	DG/UX
Compiler	Gnu C 1.96.4	gcc 2.2.2	Gnu C 2.3.3	Gnu C 2.3.3

System Performance: Buyer's Guide

	Data General AViiON 5225	Data General AViiON 5240	Data General AViiON 6240	Data General AViiON 6280
AIM Performance Rating	49.2	92.1	89.4	175.3
Maximum User Load	475	879	868	1686
Price	$43,205	$83,105	$106,393	$205,347
CPU Type	88100 (2)	88100 (4)	88100 (4)	88100 (8)
Clock Rate	25 MHz	25 MHz	25 MHz	25 MHz
External CPU Cache	32K data, 64K inst per cpu	64K data, 64K inst per cpu	64K data, 64K inst per cpu	64K/64K per cpu 1MB/cpu pair
Floating Point	Integrated	Integrated	Integrated	Integrated
RAM	64 MB	192 MB	192 MB	256 MB
Disks	520 MB, 12ms	520 MB, 12ms	1.4 GB, 15ms	520 MB, 12ms (2)
Disk Controllers	SCSI	Ciprico SCSI	Ciprico SCSI	Ciprico SCSI
I/O Buffers	Dynamic	Dynamic	Dynamic	Dynamic
O/S	DG/UX 5.4.2	DG/UX 5.4 R2.01	DG/UX 5.4.2	DG/UX 5.4R2.01E01
File System	DG/UX	DG/UX	DG/UX	DG/UX
Compiler	Gnu C 2.2.2	Gnu C 2.2.2	Gnu C 2.2.2	Gnu C 2.2.2

	Data General AViiON 8500 Quad Processor	Data General AViiON 9000 Series	Datapoint 4700 Series	DEC 2000 Model 300
AIM Performance Rating	132.2	456.6	33.1	68.6
Maximum User Load	1271	4286	279	178
Price	$77,945	$268,551	$34,286	$11,798
CPU Type	88110 (4)	88110-L5 (8)	80486 (2)	21064
Clock Rate	45 MHz	50 MHz	33 MHz	150 MHz
External CPU Cache	8k data, 8k inst 1st 256k 2nd	8K data/8K inst 1st 1MB/cpu 2nd	256K per cpu	64 KB
Floating Point	Integrated	Integrated	Integrated	Integrated
RAM	192 MB	608 MB	64 MB	64 MB
Disks	520 MB, 12ms (3)	520 MB, 8.5ms (4)	420 MB, 16ms(1) 663 MB, 15.5ms (1)	1.3 GB, 9ms (2)
Disk Controllers	Integrated SCSI	Integrated SCSI	EISA SCSI	SCSI
I/O Buffers	Dynamic	Dynamic	Dynamic	Dynamic
O/S	DG/UX 5.4R2.10.4.1e01	DG/UX 5.4R3.00	SVR4 3.1	DEC OSF/1 V1.3b
File System	DG/UX	DG/UX	UFS	UFS
Compiler	Gnu C 2.3.3.2	Gnu C 2.4.5	ATT ANSI C 5.0	DEC OSF/1 AXP C V1.3

System Performance: Buyer's Guide

	DEC 3000 Model 300L	DEC 3000 Model 400S	DEC 3000 Model 500S	DEC 3000 Model 600S
AIM Performance Rating	42	70.3	82.9	93.8
Maximum User Load	225	485	649	537
Price	$8,695	$27,504	$53,088	$38,609
CPU Type	21064	21064	21064	21064
Clock Rate	100 MHz	133 MHz	150 MHz	175 MHz
External CPU Cache	256K	512K	512K	2 MB
Floating Point	Integrated	Integrated	Integrated	Integrated
RAM	64 MB	128 MB	192 MB	128 MB
Disks	1.3 GB, 9ms	1.3 GB, 9.5ms(2) 426 MB, 14ms	1.3 GB, 9ms(2) 426 MB, 14.5ms(6)	1.3 GB, 9ms (3)
Disk Controllers	Integrated SCSI	Int SCSI + SCSI	Integrated SCSI (2)	SCSI (2)
I/O Buffers	Dynamic	Dynamic	Dynamic + 1M PrestoServe	Dynamic
O/S	DEC OSF/1 X1.3 (Rev 10.411)	DEC OSF/1 V1.2 (Rev 9)	DEC OSF/1 V1.2 (Rev 9)	DEC OSF/1 T2.0-2 (Rev 146)
File System	UFS	UFS	UFS	UFS
Compiler	DEC OSF/1 AXP C X1.3.0308	DEC C v3.11	DEC C v3.11	DEC OSF/1 AXP C T2.0

	DEC 3000 Model 800S	DEC 4000 Model 610	DEC 4000 Model 710	DEC applicationDEC 400XP
AIM Performance Rating	119.3	92	105.1	27.7
Maximum User Load	902	655	776	230
Price	$93,844	$94,776	$113,848	$17,472
CPU Type	21064	21064	21064	80486
Clock Rate	200 MHz	160 MHz	190 MHz	50 MHz
External CPU Cache	2 MB	1 MB	4 MB	256K
Floating Point	Integrated	Integrated	Integrated	Integrated
RAM	384 MB	512 MB	512 MB	64 MB
Disks	1.3 GB, 9ms (4)	1.3 GB, 9ms (3)	1.3 GB, 9ms (3)	426 MB,14ms(2)
Disk Controllers	SCSI (2)	SCSI	SCSI	Adaptec SCSI
I/O Buffers	Dynamic + 1 MB PrestoServe	Dynamic + 4 MB PrestoServe	Dynamic + 4 MB PrestoServe	36752 KB
O/S	DEC OSF/1 T2.0-2 (Rev 146)	DEC OSF/1 V1.3 (Rev 111)	DEC OSF/1 V1.3 (Rev 111)	SCO Sys V/386 3.2V4s
File System	UFS	UFS	UFS	EAFS
Compiler	DEC OSF/1 AXP C T2.0	DEC OSF/1 AXP C V1.3	DEC OSF/1 AXP C V1.3	SCO C 3.2.2t

System Performance: Buyer's Guide

	DECpc 450ST	DECstation 5000 Model 240	DECsystem 5000 Model 25	DECsystem 5000 Model 50
AIM Performance Rating	27.7	33.1	15.3	41.4
Maximum User Load	230	249	136	167
Price	$13,144	$34,100	$13,715	$16,895
CPU Type	80486	R3000A	R3000A	R4000
Clock Rate	50 MHz	40 MHz	25MHz	50 MHz
External CPU Cache	256K	64K data, 64K inst	64K data, 64K inst	1024K
Floating Point	Integrated	R3010	R3010	Integrated
RAM	64 MB	96 MB	40 MB	40 MB
Disks	426 MB, 14ms(2)	426 MB, 14ms(2)	426 MB, 16 ms(2)	425 MB, 14.5ms (3)
Disk Controllers	Adaptec SCSI	Integral SCSI	Integral SCSI	Integrated SCSI
I/O Buffers	36752 KB	48 MB	20 MB	16 MB
O/S	SCO Sys V/386 3.2V4s	ULTRIX v4.2a	ULTRIX 4.2a	ULTRIX T4.3A-5 (Rev 116)
File System	EAFS	FFS	FFS	FFS
Compiler	SCO C 3.2.2t	MIPS C 2.1	MIPS C 2.1	MIPS C 3.0

	DECsystem 5000 Model 260	DECsystem 5900	Diab Data DIAB2440	Diab Data DS90-45
AIM Performance Rating	70.1	33.2	23.6	88.9
Maximum User Load	328	281	163	668
Price	$37,095	$78,600	$37,600	$145,000
CPU Type	R4400	R3000A	MC68040	MC68040 (4)
Clock Rate	60 MHz	40 MHz	33 MHz	33 MHz
External CPU Cache	16K data, 16K inst 1st 1024K 2nd lvl	64K data, 64K inst	none	64K
Floating Point	Integrated	R3010	Integrated	Integrated
RAM	128 MB	128 MB	64 MB	128 MB
Disks	1.0 GB, 12.5ms (2) 426 MB, 14.5ms (2)	1.3 GB, 12.5ms(2); 1.0 GB, 14.5ms(2)	600 MB, 15ms	1 GB, 15ms(3)
Disk Controllers	Integrated SCSI	Integral SCSI (1); Turbochannel SCSI (2)	Proprietary SCSI	Proprietary SCSI (3)
I/O Buffers	64 MB	64 MB	Dynamic	Dynamic
O/S	ULTRIX v4.3A (Rev 139)	ULTRIX 4.2a	D-NIX 5.3.2.3	D-NIX 5.3 2.3
File System	FFS	FFS	fh00	fh00
Compiler	MIPS C 3.0	MIPS C 2.1	D-CC 2.37c	D-CC 2.37c

System Performance: Buyer's Guide

	Diab Data DS90-47	Encore Infinity 90 (Model 40 - 16 CPU)	Encore Infinity 90 (Model 40 - 24 CPU)	Encore 91 Series (4 CPU, 128K)
AIM Performance Rating	143.1	238.5	366.8	59.9
Maximum User Load	1123	2220	2973	505
Price	$121,000	$714,388	$993,988	$107,663
CPU Type	MC68040 (6)	88100 (16)	88100 (24)	88100 (4)
Clock Rate	33 MHz	25 MHz	25 MHz	25 MHz
External CPU Cache	128K/cpu	512K total	32K per cpu	16K data, 16K inst per cpu
Floating Point	Integrated	Integrated	Integrated	Integrated
RAM	256 MB	512 MB	768 MB	128 MB
Disks	600 MB, 15ms 1 GB, 15ms	1.2 GB, 18ms(24)	600 MB, 18ms(30)	600 MB, 18 ms (4)
Disk Controllers	Proprietary SCSI (2)	SCSI (8) VME SCSI (16)	Single Ended SCSI (6), Differential SCSI (6)	Encore SCSI (2)
I/O Buffers	Dynamic	132 MB	270 MB	68 MB
O/S	D-NIX 5.3 2.3A	Umax 3.0.6.7	Umax 3.0.7	Umax 3.0.6.7
File System	fh00	BSD	BSD	BSD Fast
Compiler	D-CC v2.37c	Encore C 1.1	Encore C 1.1.2a	Encore C 1.1

	Encore 91 Series (4 CPU, 512K)	Hewlett-Packard 9000 Model 705	Hewlett-Packard 9000 Model 710	Hewlett-Packard 9000 Model 712/60
AIM Performance Rating	67.1	20	29.6	44.5
Maximum User Load	583	134	180	170
Price	$129,487	$8,840	$14,490	$5,400
CPU Type	MC88100 (4)	PA-RISC 1.1	PA-RISC 1.1	PA 7100LC
Clock Rate	25 MHz	35 MHz	50 MHz	60 MHz
External CPU Cache	128K per cpu	64K data, 32 K inst	64K data, 32K inst	64K
Floating Point	Integrated	Custom 35 MHz	Custom 50 MHz	Integrated
RAM	128 MB	16 MB	16 MB	16 MB
Disks	600 MB, 18 ms (5)	420 MB, 13ms	420 MB, 13ms (2)	525 MB, 13ms
Disk Controllers	SCSI (2)	NCR53C700 SCSI	NCR SCSI 53C700	Integrated SCSI II
I/O Buffers	53 MB	6 MB	6 MB	Dynamic
O/S	Umax 3.0.7	HP-UX 8.07	HPUX 8.05	HP-UX 9.03
File System	BSD	FFS	Berkeley FFS	BFS
Compiler	Encore C 1.1.2a	HP C A.08.71	HP92453 rev.A.08.54	HP 92453 v10.03

System Performance: Buyer's Guide

	Hewlett-Packard 9000 712/80i	Hewlett-Packard 9000 Model 715/33	Hewlett-Packard 9000 Model 715/50	Hewlett-Packard 9000 Series 700 Model 715/75
AIM Performance Rating	64.1	21.8	33.7	63
Maximum User Load	310	143	252	125
Price	$10,380	$7,995	$19,100	$15,490
CPU Type	PA7100LC	PA-RISC 7100	PA-RISC 7100	PA-RISC 7100
Clock Rate	80 MHz	33 MHz	50 MHz	75 MHz
External CPU Cache	256K	64K data, 64K inst	64K data, 64K inst	256K data, 256K inst
Floating Point	Integrated	Integrated	Integrated	Integrated
RAM	32 MB	16 MB	32 MB	32 MB
Disks	1 GB, 11.5ms	525 MB, 13ms (1)	1 GB, 11.5ms (2)	1.0 GB, 10ms
Disk Controllers	Integrated SCSI II	Integrated SCSI	Integrated SCSI	SCSI
I/O Buffers	Dynamic	Dynamic	Dynamic	Dynamic
O/S	HP-UX 9.03	HP-UX 9.0	HP-UX 9.0	HP-UX 9.01
File System	BFS	BFS	BFS	HFS
Compiler	HP 92453 v10.03	cc A.09.16	cc A.09.19	HP C A.09.34

	Hewlett-Packard 9000 Model 725/50	Hewlett-Packard 9000 Model 725/50	Hewlett-Packard 9000 Model 735	Hewlett-Packard 9000 Model 750
AIM Performance Rating	34.2	34	71.7	46.7
Maximum User Load	246	301	422	388
Price	$18,000	$26,700	$41,800	$57,995
CPU Type	PA-RISC 7100	PA-RISC 7100	PA-RISC 7100	PA-RISC 1.1
Clock Rate	50 MHz	50 MHz	99 MHz	66 MHz
External CPU Cache	64K data, 64K inst	64K data, 64K inst	256K data, 256K inst	256K data, 256K inst
Floating Point	Integrated	Integrated	Integrated	Custom 66 MHz
RAM	32 MB	64 MB	32 MB	64 MB
Disks	525 MB, 13ms	1 GB, 11.5ms (2)	1 GB, 11.5ms (2)	1.3 GB, 13ms (2)
Disk Controllers	Integrated SCSI-2	Integrated SCSI-2	Integrated SCSI II	Integrated SCSI
I/O Buffers	Dynamic	Dynamic	Dynamic	Dynamic
O/S	HP-UX 9.01	HP-UX 9.01	HP-UX 9.01	HP-UX 9.0
File System	BFS	BFS	BFS	BFS
Compiler	cc ver 09.19	cc ver 09.19	cc A.09.19	cc A.09.19

System Performance: Buyer's Guide

	Hewlett-Packard 9000 Model 755	Hewlett-Packard 9000 Model 800 H70	Hewlett-Packard 9000 Model E25	Hewlett-Packard 9000 Model G50
AIM Performance Rating	71.7	140	44.5	69.2
Maximum User Load	580	1024	392	620
Price	$68,800	$293,099	$44,494	$111,945
CPU Type	PA-RISC 7100	PA-RISC 7100 (2)	PA-RISC 7100LC	HP-PA 7100
Clock Rate	99 MHz	96 MHz	48 MHz	96 MHz
External CPU Cache	256K data, 256K inst	2M data, 2M inst	64K	256K data, 256K inst
Floating Point	Integrated	Integrated	Integrated	HP-PA 7100
RAM	64 MB	256 MB	128 MB	256 MB
Disks	2GB, 11.5ms (2)	1.3 GB, 13.5ms (21)	1.0 GB, 10.5ms (2) 1.0 GB, 10.5ms (7)	1.3 GB, 13.5ms (9)
Disk Controllers	Integ SCSI II	SCSI, PBA-FL (2)	Internal SE SCSI HP-PB FW SCSI	HP SCSI (3)
I/O Buffers	Dynamic	90 MB	64 MB	80 MB
O/S	HP-UX 9.01	HP-UX 9.0	HP-UX 9.04	HP-UX 9.0
File System	BFS	BSD	BSD	BSD
Compiler	cc A.09.19	cc A.09.19	HP C X.10.03	cc A.09.19

	Hewlett-Packard 9000 Model G50	Hewlett-Packard 9000 Model T500	IBM RISC System/6000 POWERserver 360	IBM RISC System/6000 POWERserver 365
AIM Performance Rating	91.4	88.7	47.7	47.7
Maximum User Load	820	775	428	428
Price	$77,745	$218,212	$40,487	$39,332
CPU Type	PA-RISC 7100	PA-RISC 7100	IBM POWER 5032	IBM POWER 5032
Clock Rate	96 MHz	90 MHz	50 MHz	50 MHz
External CPU Cache	256K data, 256K inst	1 MB data 1 MB inst	32K data, 32K inst	32K data, 32K inst
Floating Point	Integrated	Integrated	Integrated	Integrated
RAM	256 MB	256 MB	128 MB	128 MB
Disks	2 GB, 11 ms (2) 1.0 GB, 10.5ms (7)	1.36 GB, 13.5ms (2) 1.0 GB, 10.5ms (10)	1 GB, 11.5ms (3)	1 GB, 11.5ms (3)
Disk Controllers	Internal SE SCSI HP-PB FW SCSI	HP-FL HP-PB FW SCSI	Integrated SCSI	Integrated SCSI
I/O Buffers	150 MB	150 MB	Dynamic	Dynamic
O/S	HP-UX 9.04	HP-UX 9.04	AIX v3.2.3	AIX v3.2.3
File System	BSD	BSD	AIX	AIX
Compiler	HP C X.10.03	HP C X.10.03	xlc v1.2.1	xlc v1.2.1

System Performance: Buyer's Guide

	IBM RISC System/6000 POWERserver 370	IBM RISC System/6000 POWERserver 375	IBM RISC System/6000 POWERserver 570	IBM RISC System/6000 POWERserver 580
AIM Performance Rating	60.9	60.9	47.7	62.1
Maximum User Load	490	490	428	518
Price	$44,707	$43,552	$55,622	$83,449
CPU Type	IBM POWER 6232	IBM POWER 6232	IBM POWER 5032	IBM POWER 6264
Clock Rate	62.5 MHz	62.5 MHz	50 MHz	62.5 MHz
External CPU Cache	32K data, 32K inst	32K data, 32K inst	32K data, 32K inst	64K data, 32K inst
Floating Point	Integrated	Integrated	Integrated	Integrated
RAM	128 MB	128 MB	128 MB	128 MB
Disks	1 GB, 11.5ms (3)	1 GB, 11.5ms (3)	1 GB, 11.5ms (3)	1 GB, 11.5ms (4)
Disk Controllers	IBM SCSI	IBM SCSI	Integrated SCSI	Integrated SCSI
I/O Buffers	Dynamic	Dynamic	Dynamic	Dynamic
O/S	AIX v3.2.3	AIX v3.2.3	AIX v3.2.3	AIX v3.2.3
File System	AIX	AIX	AIX	AIX
Compiler	xlc v1.2	xlc v1.2	xlc v1.2.1	xlc v1.2

	IBM RISC System/6000 POWERserver 580H	IBM RISC System/6000 POWERserver 590	IBM RISC System/6000 POWERserver 970	IBM RISC System/6000 POWERserver 980B
AIM Performance Rating	63.3	103.6	49.9	62.1
Maximum User Load	582	803	454	518
Price	$77,754	$97,354	$115,380	$117,450
CPU Type	IBM POWER2	IBM POWER2	IBM POWER 5064	IBM POWER 6264
Clock Rate	55 MHz	66.6 MHz	50 MHz	62.5 MHz
External CPU Cache	256K data, 32K inst	32K inst, 256K data	64K data, 32K inst	64K data, 32K inst
Floating Point	Integrated	Integrated	Integrated	Integrated
RAM	192 MB	128 MB	128 MB	128 MB
Disks	IBM 2.0 GB, 11.5ms	IBM 2.0 GB, 11.5ms (4)	1.3 GB, 12ms (3)	1 GB, 11.5ms (4)
Disk Controllers	SCSI	SCSI	IBM SCSI	Integrated SCSI
I/O Buffers	Dynamic	Dynamic	Dynamic	Dynamic
O/S	AIX Version 3.2.5	AIX Version 3.2.5 Beta	AIX v3.2.1	AIX v3.2.3
File System	AIX/JFS	AIX/JFS	AIX	AIX
Compiler	xlc v1.3	xlc v1.3	xlc v1.2	xlc v1.2

System Performance: Buyer's Guide

	IBM RISC System/6000 POWERstation 250	ICL DRS 6000 Level 340	ICL DRS 6000 Level 360	ICL DRS 6000 Level 370
AIM Performance Rating	50.5	26	50.7	56.1
Maximum User Load	421	248	479	516
Price	$15,219	$12,750	$23,600	$29,900
CPU Type	POWER PC 601	SPARC	SuperSPARC	SuperSPARC
Clock Rate	66.67 MHz	40 MHz	36 MHz	40 MHz
External CPU Cache	32K	64K	16K data, 20K inst 1 MB 2nd lvl	36K 1st level 1 MB 2nd level
Floating Point	Integrated	Integrated	Integrated	Integrated
RAM	96 MB	32 MB	64 MB	96 MB
Disks	IBM 1.0 GB, 11.5ms	1.2 GB, 10.5ms	1.2 GB, 10.5ms (2)	1.2 GB, 10.5ms (2)
Disk Controllers	SCSI	Integrated SCSI-2	Integrated SCSI-2	Integrated SCSI-2
I/O Buffers	Dynamic	Dynamic	Dynamic	Dynamic
O/S	AIX Version 3.2.5	SVR 4.2 v710i8	SVR 4.2 v710i4	SVR 4.2 V710i5+
File System	AIX/JFS	VJFS	VJFS	VJFS
Compiler	xlc v1.3	GNU C v2.2.2	GNU C v2.2.2	GNU C v2.2.2

	ICL DRS 6000 Level 372	ICL DRS 6000 Level 380	ICL DRS 6000 Level 382	ICL DRS 6000 Level 450
AIM Performance Rating	93.4	71	111	41.7
Maximum User Load	846	642	1025	397
Price	$50,680	$30,055	$46,710	$54,765
CPU Type	SuperSPARC (2)	SuperSPARC	SuperSPARC (2)	SPARC (2)
Clock Rate	40 MHz	50 MHz	50 MHz	40 MHz
External CPU Cache	16K data, 20K inst/cpu 1 MB 2nd lvl	16K data, 20K inst 1st 1 MB 2nd lvl	16K data, 20K inst 1st 1 MB 2nd lvl	128K
Floating Point	Integrated	Integrated	Integrated	Integrated
RAM	128 MB	96 MB	128 MB	64 MB
Disks	1.2 GB, 10.5ms (2)	1.2 GB, 10.5ms (2)	1.2 GB, 10.5ms (2)	1.2 GB, 10.5ms (3)
Disk Controllers	Integrated SCSI-2	Integrated SCSI	Integrated SCSI	Jaguar SCSI-2 (2)
I/O Buffers	Dynamic	Dynamic	Dynamic	Dynamic
O/S	SVR 4.2 v710i5+	SVR 4.2 v711i2	SVR 4.2 v711i2	DRS/NX V6 L2 I3
File System	VJFS	VxFS	VxFS	UFS
Compiler	GNU C v2.2.2	GNU C v2.3.3	GNU C v2.3.3	Gnu C v2.2.2

System Performance: Buyer's Guide

	ICL DRS 6000 Level 752	ICL DRS 6000 Level 764	ICL FX486/33	ICL MX486/50
AIM Performance Rating	59.6	72	14.4	24.9
Maximum User Load	558	660	135	237
Price	$96,500	$129,200	$16,417	$30,604
CPU Type	SPARC (4)	SuperSPARC (4)	80486	80486
Clock Rate	40 MHz	33 MHz	33 MHz	50 MHz
External CPU Cache	64K per cpu 1 MB /cpu pair	36K per cpu 1 MB per cpu	128K	256K
Floating Point	Integrated	Integrated	Integrated	Integrated
RAM	128 MB	128 MB	32 MB	64 MB
Disks	1.2 GB, 10.5ms (4)	1.2 GB, 10.5ms (6)	425 MB, 14ms (3)	1.2 GB, 14ms (2) 400 MB, 15.7ms (2)
Disk Controllers	Jaguar2 SCSI-2 (2)	Jaguar SCSI-2 (4)	Adaptec SCSI	Adaptec 1740A SCSI
I/O Buffers	Dynamic	Dynamic	8 MB	Dynamic
O/S	DRS/NX V6L2I3	DRS/NX V6.0 L2I3	SCO UNIX 3.2 v4.2	DRS/NX SVR4 PC V6 L1
File System	UFS	UFS	AFS	UFS
Compiler	GNU C 2.2.2	GNU C v2.2.2	SCO C 3.2 v4/2.0	AT&T v5.0

	Motorola Delta Series 4220	Motorola Series 900 Model M921	Motorola Series 900 Model M922	Motorola Series 8000 Model M8120
AIM Performance Rating	20.1	59.2	53.3	18.1
Maximum User Load	179	199	506	172
Price	$13,367	$20,662	$26,257	$10,932
CPU Type	68040	MC88110	MC88110	88100
Clock Rate	25 MHz	50 MHz	50 MHz	25 MHz
External CPU Cache	none	none	none	32K
Floating Point	Integrated	Integrated	Integrated	Integrated
RAM	32 MB	32 MB	64 MB	32 MB
Disks	520 MB, 12 ms	520 MB, 12ms	330 MB, 12ms (2)	520 MB, 12ms
Disk Controllers	SCSI	Integrated SCSI	Integrated SCSI	SCSI
I/O Buffers	14 MB	Dynamic	Dynamic	13 MB
O/S	SYSTEM V/68 R3V7	Sys V/88 R40v4.2	Sys V/88 R40v4.2	SYSTEM V/88 R32V3
File System	SYSTEM V enhanced	UFS	UFS	SYSV Enhanced
Compiler	GNU-C	Gnu C v2.2	Gnu C v2.2	Green Hills v1.8.5

System Performance: Buyer's Guide

	Motorola Series 8000 Model 8220	Motorola Series 8000 Model M8540	Motorola Series 8000 Model M8540	Motorola Series 8000 Model M8640 (4 CPU, 2 Disk)
AIM Performance Rating	23.7	87.6	88.8	62
Maximum User Load	225	146	826	428
Price	$16,767	$55,967	$102,967	$60,737
CPU Type	88100	88100 (4)	88100 (4)	88100 (4)
Clock Rate	33 MHz	25 MHz	25 MHz	25 MHz
External CPU Cache	32K	256K inst, 256K data	256Kinst. 256Kdata	128 KB
Floating Point	Integrated	Integrated	Integrated	Integrated
RAM	48 MB	16 MB	256 MB	96 MB
Disks	520 MB, 12ms	1.0 GB, 12ms	1.0 GB, 12ms	1 GB, 15 ms (2)
Disk Controllers	Integrated SCSI	SCSI	SCSI	Motorola SCSI
I/O Buffers	20 MB	7 MB	154 MB	46 MB
O/S	Sys V/88 R32v3.1	Sys V/88 R32v3.2	Sys V/88 R32v3.2	SYSTEM V/88 R32V2
File System	Sys V Enhanced	Sys V Enhanced	Sys V Enhanced	SYSTEM V Enhanced
Compiler	Green Hills v1.8.5	Diab Data D-CC/88K V3.0d	Diab Data D-CC/88K V3.0d	Green Hills v1.8.5

	Motorola Series 8000 Model M8640 (4 CPU, 4 Disk)	NCR StarServer E Release 2	NCR StarServer E Release 2	NCR System 3000 Model 3345
AIM Performance Rating	62.4	16.7	59.4	17.6
Maximum User Load	561	158	527	140
Price	$95,927	$53,504	$169,470	$12,014
CPU Type	88100 (4)	80486	80486 (4)	80486
Clock Rate	25 MHz	33 MHz	33 MHz	33 MHz
External CPU Cache	128 KB	256K	256K	(none)
Floating Point	Integrated (4)	Integrated	Integrated	Integrated
RAM	256 MB	48 MB	128 MB	16 MB dual-ported
Disks	1 GB, 15 ms (4)	327 MB, 19ms (2) 608 MB, 19ms (1) 200 MB, 20ms (2)	327 MB, 19ms (1) 200 MB, 20ms (23) 1001 MB, 18ms (1)	200 MB, 15ms (2)
Disk Controllers	MOTOROLA SCSI MVME 328-1	EISA SCSI	EISA SCSI (6)	NCR SCSI 53C700
I/O Buffers	145 MB	Dynamic	Dynamic	Dynamic
O/S	SYSTEM V/88 R32V3	SVR 4.0 V3.0 (SMP)	SVR 4.0 V3.0 (SMP)	NCR SVR4 r1.00
File System	SYS V Enhanced	UFS	UFS	UFS
Compiler	Green Hills v1.8.5	AT&T CI 5.0	AT&T CI 5.0	cc r1.01

System Performance: Buyer's Guide

	NCR System 3000 Model 3445	NCR System 3000 Model 3447	NCR System 3000 Model 3450	NCR System 3000 Model 3450
AIM Performance Rating	17.8	25.6	26.7	49.4
Maximum User Load	148	212	222	400
Price	$23,149	$28,105	$60,040	$88,740
CPU Type	80486	80486	80486	80486 (2)
Clock Rate	33 MHz	50 MHz	50 MHz	50 MHz
External CPU Cache	(none)	128K	256K	256K per cpu
Floating Point	Integrated	Integrated	Integrated	Integrated
RAM	32 MB dual-ported	32 MB	64 MB	128 MB
Disks	670 MB, 18ms (2)	670 MB, 18ms (2)	1.3 GB, 11.5ms (2)	1.3 GB, 11.5ms (3)
Disk Controllers	NCR SCSI 53C700	NCR SCSI 53C700	NCR SCSI 53C700	NCR SCSI 53C700
I/O Buffers	Dynamic	Dynamic	Dynamic	Dynamic
O/S	NCR SVR4 r1.00	NCR SVR4 r1.01	SVR4 r2.00	SVR4 r2.00
File System	UFS	UFS	UFS	UFS
Compiler	cc r1.01	cc r1.01	cc r1.01	cc r1.01

	NetFRAME NF250CS	Olivetti LSX 5015	Olivetti LSX 5025 Enhanced	Olivetti LSX 5030/2
AIM Performance Rating	71	19.1	28.9	27.6
Maximum User Load	522	181	275	258
Price	$59,908	$12,535	$11,349	$42,208
CPU Type	Pentium	80486DX2	80486DX2	80486DX (2)
Clock Rate	66 MHz	25/50 MHz	33/66 MHz	33 MHz
External CPU Cache	256K	none	128K	256K per cpu
Floating Point	Integrated	Integrated	Integrated	Integrated
RAM	128 MB	32 MB	48 MB	64 MB
Disks	550 MB, 11ms (3) 1.05 GB, 11ms	340 MB, 12ms	340 MB, 14ms	Seagate 340 MB. 12 ms
Disk Controllers	SCSI-II	ESC2 SCSI	Dual Channel SCSI	ESC2 SCSI
I/O Buffers	Dynamic	Dynamic	Dynamic	Dynamic
O/S	UnixWare V1.0	SVR4.0 v2.1	SVR4.0 v2.2.1	SVR4.0 v2.1
File System	VXFS	UFS	UFS	UFS
Compiler	UnixWare V1.0 SDK (Rev. A)	AT&T C	AT&T C	AT&T C

System Performance: Buyer's Guide

	Olivetti LSX 5030/3	Olivetti LSX 5040 Enhanced	Olivetti LSX 5040/2 Enhanced	Olivetti LSX 5040/3 Enhanced
AIM Performance Rating	40.4	36.2	60.8	88.8
Maximum User Load	367	332	559	771
Price	$61,596	$23,079	$31,174	$37,854
CPU Type	80486DX (3)	80486DX2	80486DX2 (2)	80486DX2 (3)
Clock Rate	33 MHz	33/66 MHz	33/66 MHz	33/66 MHz
External CPU Cache	256K per cpu	1 MB	1 MB	1 MB
Floating Point	Integrated	Integrated	Integrated	Integrated
RAM	96 MB	48 MB	96 MB	128 MB
Disks	Seagate 340 MB. 12 ms (2)	525 MB, 14ms	525 MB, 14ms (2)	525 MB, 14ms (2)
Disk Controllers	ESC2 SCSI	ESC2 SCSI	ESC2 SCSI	ESC2 SCSI
I/O Buffers	Dynamic	Dynamic	Dynamic	Dynamic
O/S	SVR4.0 v2.1	SVR4.0 v2.2.1	SVR4.0 v2.2.1 MP	SVR4.0 v2.2.1 MP
File System	UFS	UFS	UFS	UFS
Compiler	AT&T C	AT&T C	AT&T C	AT&T C

	Olivetti LSX 5040/4 Enhanced	Pyramid MIServer-S 12/6	Pyramid MIServer-S 12/8	Pyramid MIServer-S 12/12
AIM Performance Rating	110.6	88.1	113.5	144.3
Maximum User Load	905	789	1000	1333
Price	$42,396	$615,750	$713,250	$927,750
CPU Type	80486DX2 (4)	R3000 (6)	R3000 (8)	R3000 (12)
Clock Rate	33/66 MHz	33 MHz	33 MHz	33 MHz
External CPU Cache	1 MB	64K data, 64K inst 1st; 4 MB unified 2nd lvl	64K data, 64K inst 1st; 4 MB unified 2nd lvl	64K data, 64K inst 1st; 4 MB unified 2nd lvl
Floating Point	Integrated	R3010 (6)	R3010 (8)	R3010 (12)
RAM	128 MB	288 MB	384 MB	512 MB
Disks	525 MB, 14ms (4)	2 GB, 12ms (6)	2 GB, 12ms (6)	2 GB, 12ms (8)
Disk Controllers	ESC2 SCSI	IPI-2 Proprietary (2)	IPI Proprietary (2)	IPI-2 Proprietary (2)
I/O Buffers	Dynamic	Dynamic	Dynamic	Dynamic
O/S	SVR4.0 v2.2.1 MP	DC/OSX v1.1-92c012; UNIX SVR4	DC/OSX v1.1-92c012 UNIX SVR4	DC/OSX v1.1-92c012 UNIX SVR4
File System	UFS	UFS	UFS	UFS
Compiler	AT&T C	cc	cc	cc

System Performance: Buyer's Guide

	Sequoia Series 400	Silicon Graphics CHALLENGE L	Silicon Graphics CHALLENGE L	Silicon Graphics Challenge M/Indigo 2
AIM Performance Rating	69.7	152.5	245.8	113.3
Maximum User Load	598	1173	1739	798
Price	$995,000	$139,100	$196,900	$30,900
CPU Type	68040 (8)	MIPS R4400 (2)	MIPS R4400 (4)	MIPS R4400SC
Clock Rate	25 MHz	75/150 MHz	75/150 MHz	75/150 MHz
External CPU Cache	256K	16K data, 16K inst-on-chip, 1 MB 2nd lvl	16K data, 16K inst-on-chip, 1 MB 2nd lvl	1 MB 2nd lvl
Floating Point	Integrated	MIPS R4010 (2)	R4010 (4)	Integrated
RAM	256 MB	256 MB	256 MB	96 MB
Disks	1.2 GB, 15ms (2)	2.0 GB, 9.4ms (4)	2.0 GB, 9.4ms (6)	1 GB, 12ms
Disk Controllers	Ciprico SCSI Rimfire 1500	Integrated SCSI-II	Integrated SCSI-II	Integrated SCSI-2
I/O Buffers	Dynamic	Dynamic	Dynamic	Dynamic
O/S	TOPIX Ver 6.5.12	IRIX 5.1	IRIX 5.1	IRIX 5.1
File System	Extent Based	EFS	EFS	EFS
Compiler	LPI ANSI C Beta	ANSI C 3.17	ANSI C 3.17	ANSI C 3.17

	Silicon Graphics Indigo R4000	Silicon Graphics Indigo R4000	Silicon Graphics Indy R4000SC	Sun SPARCcenter 1000
AIM Performance Rating	71	72	71	138.2
Maximum User Load	289	497	442	1149
Price	$16,485	$22,485	$14,495	$80,500
CPU Type	MIPS R4000SC	MIPS R4000SC	MIPS R4000SC	SuperSPARC (4)
Clock Rate	50/100 MHz	50/100 MHz	50/100 MHz	50 MHz
External CPU Cache	1 MB	1 MB	1 MB	36K/cpu 1st 1 MB/cpu 2nd lvl
Floating Point	Integrated	Integrated	Integrated	Integrated
RAM	32 MB	96 MB	48 MB	128 MB
Disks	432 MB	432 MB	535 MB, 12ms	535 MB, 12 ms (6)
Disk Controllers	Integrated SCSI-2	Integrated SCSI-2	Integrated SCSI-II	Integrated FSBE (2)
I/O Buffers	Dynamic	Dynamic	Dynamic	Dynamic +4 MB PrestoServe
O/S	IRIX 4.0.5	IRIX 4.0.5	IRIX 5.1	Solaris 2.3
File System	EFS	EFS	EFS	UFS
Compiler	ANSI C 3.10	ANSI C 3.10	ANSI C 3.17	SC 2.0.1

System Performance: Buyer's Guide

	Sun SPARCcenter 2000	Sun SPARCclassic	Sun SPARCserver 2	Sun SPARCserver 10 Model 30
AIM Performance Rating	259.5	18.1	15.4	37
Maximum User Load	1969	140	142	159
Price	$293,735	$4,820	$14,495	$21,495
CPU Type	SuperSPARC (8)	SPARC	SPARC SS2	SuperSPARC
Clock Rate	50 MHz	50 MHz	40 MHz	36 MHz
External CPU Cache	36K/cpu 1st 2 MB/cpu 2nd lvl	6K	64 KB	32K
Floating Point	Integrated	Integrated	Integrated	Integrated
RAM	384 MB	24 MB	32 MB	48 MB
Disks	2.1 GB, 11ms (12)	207 MB, 12ms	424 MB, 11.5ms (2)	424 MB, 11.5ms (3)
Disk Controllers	DSCSI (4)	Integrated SCSI-2	SUN SCSI	Integrated SCSI
I/O Buffers	Dynamic +8 MB PrestoServe	Dynamic	Dynamic	Dynamic
O/S	Solaris 2.3	Solaris 2.2	SUN OS 4.1.1	SunOS 4.1.3
File System	UFS	UFS	BSD	UFS
Compiler	SC 2.0.1	SC 2.0.1	SPARC C 1.1	Sun C 2.0.1

	Sun SPARCserver 10 Model 40	Sun SPARCserver 10 Model 41	Sun SPARCserver 10 Model 51	Sun SPARCserver 10 Model 512
AIM Performance Rating	38.6	43.3	52.9	96.2
Maximum User Load	209	329	347	814
Price	$15,495	$21,745	$24,345	$38,770
CPU Type	SuperSPARC	SuperSPARC	SuperSPARC	SuperSPARC (2)
Clock Rate	40 MHz	40 MHz	50 MHz	50 MHz
External CPU Cache	36K	36K 1st, 1 MB 2nd	36K 1st, 1MB 2nd	36K 1st, 1 MB 2nd
Floating Point	Integrated	Integrated	Integrated	Integrated
RAM	32 MB	64 MB	64 MB	112 MB
Disks	1.05 GB, 11 ms	1.05 GB, 11 ms (2)	1.05 GB, 11ms 535 MB, 11ms	535 MB, 11ms 1.05 GB, 11 ms (2)
Disk Controllers	Integrated SCSI-2	Integrated SCSI-2	Integrated SCSI	Integrated SCSI-2
I/O Buffers	Dynamic	Dynamic	Dynamic	Dynamic 1 MB PrestoServe
O/S	Solaris 1.1	Solaris 1.1	Solar is 1.1	Solaris 2.3
File System	UFS	UFS	UFS	UFS
Compiler	SC 2.0.1	SC 2.0.1	SC 2.0.1	SC 2.0.1

System Performance: Buyer's Guide

	Sun SPARCserver 630MP	Sun SPARCserver 690MP	Sun SPARCstation ELC	Sun SPARCstation IPX
AIM Performance Rating	31.7	51.3	11.3	14.4
Maximum User Load	291	409	69	117
Price	$55,095	$98,500	$5,695	$10,195
CPU Type	SPARC (2)	SPARC (4)	SPARC ELC	SPARC IPX
Clock Rate	40 MHz	40 MHz	33 MHz	40 MHz
External CPU Cache	64K	64K per CPU	none	64 KB
Floating Point	Integrated	Integrated	Integrated	Integrated
RAM	128 MB	128 MB	8 MB	16 MB
Disks	1.3 GB, 12.5ms (3)	1.3 GB, 11.5ms (4)	424 MB, 11.5ms	207 MB, 15 ms 424 MB, 11.5ms
Disk Controllers	SBE SCSI Integrated SCSI	IPI (3)	SUN SCSI	SUN SCSI
I/O Buffers	Dynamic	Dynamic	Dynamic	Dynamic
O/S	SunOS 4.1.2	SunOS 4.1.2	SUN OS 4.1.1	SUN OS 4.1.1
File System	FFS	BSD	BSD	BSD
Compiler	Sun CC 1.1	SPARC C 1.1	SPARC C 1.1	SPARC C 1.1

	Tandem Integrity S300	Tricord ES5000	Unisys U6000 Model 65	Unisys U6000 Model 65
AIM Performance Rating	16.8	125.7	24.4	47.1
Maximum User Load	162	1078	239	461
Price	$221,070	$219,090	$34,450	$47,950
CPU Type	MIPS R3000	80486 (6)	80486	80486 (2)
Clock Rate	25 MHz	33/66 MHz	50 MHz	50 MHz
External CPU Cache	128 KB	256K/cpu	1 MB	1 MB per cpu
Floating Point	MIPS R3100	Integrated	Integrated	Integrated
RAM	48 MB	256 MB	32 MB	64 MB
Disks	650 MB, 15.5ms (4)	500 MB, 11ms (1) 1.0 GB, 11ms (16) RAID/Hot Replaceable	340 MB, 14ms (2)	340 MB, 14ms (2)
Disk Controllers	Jaguar SCSI (2)	Tricord ISS SCSI	Unisys SCSI	Unisys SCSI
I/O Buffers	Dynamic	85 MB	Dynamic	Dynamic
O/S	NonStop-UX v5.4	SCO 3.2.4 MPX 3.0	SVR4 rel 1.1	SVR4 rel 1.1
File System	Veritas	EAFS	UFS	UFS
Compiler	MIPS 3.0	Metaware HighC v2.32	AT&T ANSI C v2.0	AT&T ANSI C v2.0

System Performance: Buyer's Guide

	Unisys U6000 Model 65	Unisys U6000 Model 65	Unisys U6000 Model 65	Wyse Series 7000i Model 760MP
AIM Performance Rating	67.2	84.9	98.1	49.7
Maximum User Load	656	826	960	429
Price	$61,450	$74,950	$83,950	$19,777
CPU Type	80486 (3)	80486 (4)	80486 (5)	486DX2 (2)
Clock Rate	50 MHz	50 MHz	50 MHz	33/66 MHz
External CPU Cache	1 MB per cpu	1 MB per cpu	1 MB per cpu	256K per cpu
Floating Point	Integrated	Integrated	Integrated	Integrated
RAM	96 MB	128 MB	128 MB	96 MB
Disks	340 MB, 14ms (1) 1.3 GB, 12ms (1)	340 MB, 14ms (1) 1.3 GB, 12ms (1)	340 MB, 14ms (1) 1.3 GB, 12ms (1)	500 MB, 10ms
Disk Controllers	Unisys SCSI	Unisys SCSI	Unisys SCSI	DPT B2 SCSI
I/O Buffers	Dynamic	Dynamic	Dynamic	Dynamic
O/S	SVR4 rel 1.1	SVR4 Rel 1.1	SVR4 rel 1.1	Wyse SVR 4.0 3.1
File System	UFS	UFS	UFS	UFS
Compiler	AT&T ANSI C v2.0	AT&T ANSI C v2.0	AT&T ANSI C v2.0	Sys V cc

	Wyse Series 7000i Model 760MP	Wyse Series 7000i Model 760MP	Wyse Series 7000i Model 760MP	Zenith Data Systems Z-Server 450DE Model 500
AIM Performance Rating	74	93.4	111	28.8
Maximum User Load	596	702	849	237
Price	$28,784	$37,161	$46,778	$10,191
CPU Type	486DX2 (3)	486DX2 (4)	486DX2 (5)	486DX
Clock Rate	33/66 MHz	33/66 MHz	33/66 MHz	50 MHz
External CPU Cache	256K per cpu	256K per cpu	256K per cpu	256K write back
Floating Point	Integrated	Integrated	Integrated	Integrated
RAM	128 MB	128 MB	192 MB	48 MB
Disks	500 MB, 10ms (3)	500 MB, 10ms (4)	500 MB, 10ms (4)	535 MB, 10.5ms (2)
Disk Controllers	DPT B2 SCSI	DPT B2 SCSI (2)	DPT B2 SCSI (2)	Adaptec SCSI
I/O Buffers	Dynamic	Dynamic	Dynamic	26 MB
O/S	Wyse SVR 4.0 3.1	Wyse SVR 4.0 3.1	Wyse SVR 4.0 3.1	SCO 3.2v4.1
File System	UFS	UFS	UFS	EAFS
Compiler	Sys V cc	Sys V cc	Sys V cc	Metaware High C 2.3.2

System Performance: Buyer's Guide

	Zenith Data Systems Z-Server EX P60E Model 1000A	Zenith Z-Server LT P60E Model 500		
AIM Performance Rating	50.7	50.7		
Maximum User Load	429	382		
Price	$19,497	$14,553		
CPU Type	Pentium	Pentium		
Clock Rate	60 MHz	60 MHz		
External CPU Cache	256K write back	256K write back		
Floating Point	Integrated	Integrated		
RAM	96 MB	64 MB		
Disks	535 MB, 10.5ms (4)	535 MB, 10.5ms (3)		
Disk Controllers	SCSI-2 RAID	SCSI-2		
I/O Buffers	32 MB	32 MB		
O/S	SCO 3.2v4.2	SCO 3.2v41		
File System	EAFS	EAFS		
Compiler	SCO Optimizing C v1.1.2	Metaware High C 2.3.2		

Workstation Performance

Workstations are used in many different types of environments. Users want to purchase workstations that will perform well in their environments. They also want value. In other words, a system that has a good price/performance ratio.

AIM uses the **AIM Workstation Benchmark - Suite VI** in conjunction with the **AIM Independent Resource Benchmark - Suite IX** to test workstation performance.

The Workstation Benchmark includes application mixes created to represent specific workstation environments:

- **General Workstation Mix**
- **Mechanical CAD/Numeric Analysis Mix**
- **GIS/Imaging Mix**
- **General Business Mix**

If the test environment does not match any of these application mixes, a custom user mix can be created that more closely represents the test environment.

The Independent Resource Benchmark measures processing rates for subsystems, I/O transfers, function calls, and UNIX system calls.

Benchmark results are used to create **Certified Workstation Reports** that detail the performance results for the selected system and application mix. The report includes two important ratings: Peak Performance, and Sustained Performance.

Peak Performance, reported in application jobs per minute, is the system's highest performance level when a significant amount of CPU, floating point, and disk caching is used. Sustained Performance is the measurement taken when the system's capacity is reached; that is, when system performance becomes unacceptable to the user.

Pages 2 - 4 of each report include performance ratings for Special Interest Areas: Job Timing Index, floating point, integer math, library routines, system calls, file system, IPC, and algorithmic functions.

Certified Workstation Report

AIM Technology

A UNIX Performance Summary Based on the AIM Workstation Benchmark and the AIM Independent Resource Benchmark (Release 1.0)
General Business Mix

Hewlett Packard 9000 Model 715

Price	*CPU Type*	*Clock Rate*	*1st Level Cache*	*2nd Level Cache*	*RAM*
N/A	PA-RISC 7100	33 MHz	8K	128K	48 MB

Disks	*Display*	*I/O Buffers*	*O/S*	*File System*	*Compiler*
CASD 2000 1.7 GB, 64 MB Cache	1024x768x8 19" Color	Dynamic	HPUX 9.01	BFS	cc A.09.16

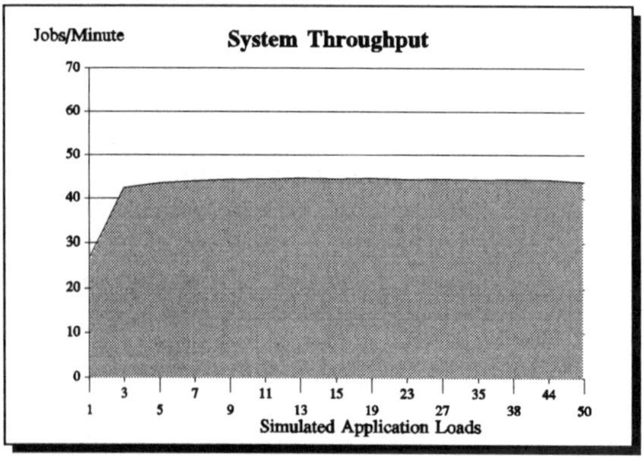

Peak Performance
44.6 AIM Business Jobs/Minute

The **Peak Performance** reflects the system throughput at the point at which the system is able to process the most jobs per minute.

Sustained Performance
43.6 AIM Business Loads

The **Sustained performance** indicates the multitasking application load where the system's performance could become unacceptable, i.e. less than 1 job/minute/AIM Business load.

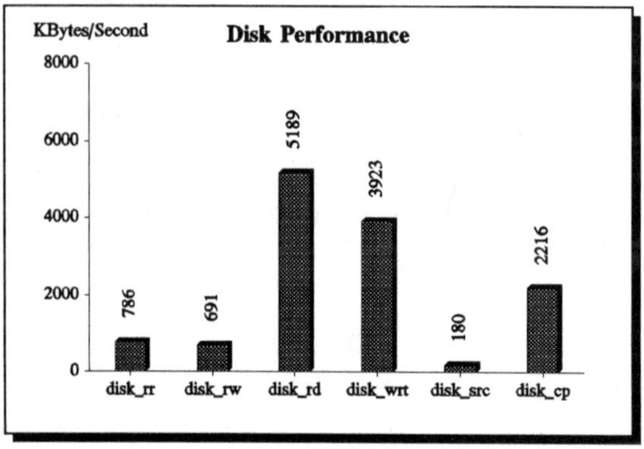

The single-tasking performance of cached disk operations (Random read/ write, Sequential read/write, directory search and copy) is represented in kilobytes per second. Cached disk performance is especially important for interactive applications such as **Software Development and Spreadsheets.**

Certified By:

AIM Technology

Date: Dec 27, 1993
S/N# 0009

Certified Workstation Report

AIM Technology

A UNIX Performance Summary Based on the AIM Workstation Benchmark and the AIM Independent Resource Benchmark (Release 1.0)

General Business Mix

IBM RISC System/6000 POWERstation 230

Price	CPU Type	Clock Rate	1st Level Cache	2nd Level Cache	RAM
N/A	Power 2508	25 MHz	8K	128K	48 MB

Disks	Display	I/O Buffers	O/S	File System	Compiler
CASD 2000 1.7 GB, 64 MB Cache	1024x768x8 19" Color	Dynamic	AIX v3.2	AIX	xlc v1.2.1

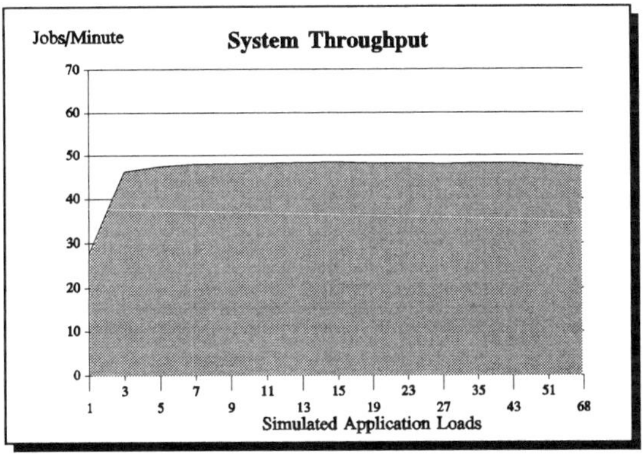

Peak Performance

48.4 AIM Business Jobs/Minute

The **Peak Performance** reflects the system throughput at the point at which the system is able to process the most jobs per minute.

Sustained Performance

47.3 AIM Business Loads

The **Sustained performance** indicates the multitasking application load where the system's performance could become unacceptable, i.e. less than 1 job/minute/AIM Business load.

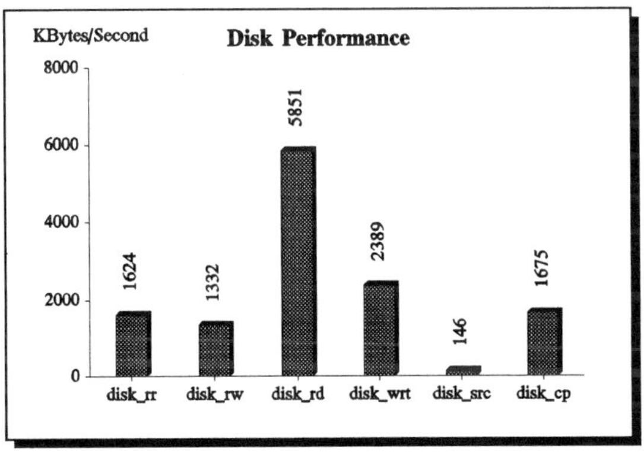

The single-tasking performance of cached disk operations (Random read/ write, Sequential read/write, directory search and copy) is represented in kilobytes per second. Cached disk performance is especially important for interactive applications such as **Software Development and Spreadsheets.**

Certified By:

AIM Technology

Date: Dec 27, 1993
S/N# 0002

Certified Workstation Report

AIM Technology

A UNIX Performance Summary Based on the AIM Workstation Benchmark and the AIM Independent Resource Benchmark (Release 1.0)
General Business Mix

SUN SPARC Classic

Price	*CPU Type*	*Clock Rate*	*1st Level Cache*	*2nd Level Cache*	*RAM*
N/A	MicroSPARC	33 MHz	8K	256K	24 MB

Disks	*Display*	*I/O Buffers*	*O/S*	*File System*	*Compiler*
500 MB, 13ms	1024x768x8 14" Mono	Dynamic	Solaris v2.1	UFS	gcc

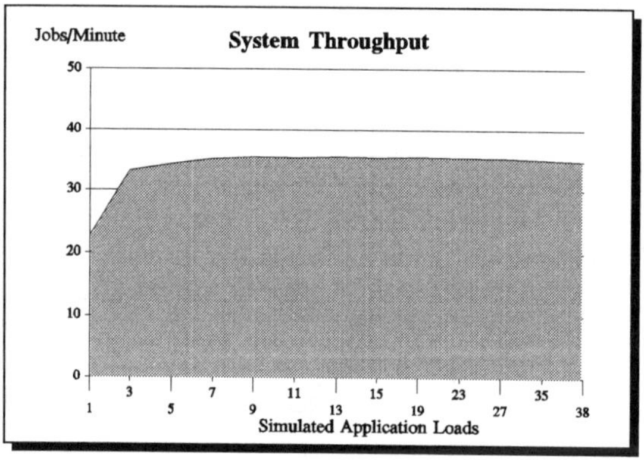

Peak Performance
35.5 AIM Business Jobs/Minute

The **Peak Performance** reflects the system throughput at the point at which the system is able to process the most jobs per minute.

Sustained Performance
34.5 AIM Business Loads

The **Sustained performance** indicates the multitasking application load where the system's performance could become unacceptable, i.e. less than 1 job/minute/AIM Business load.

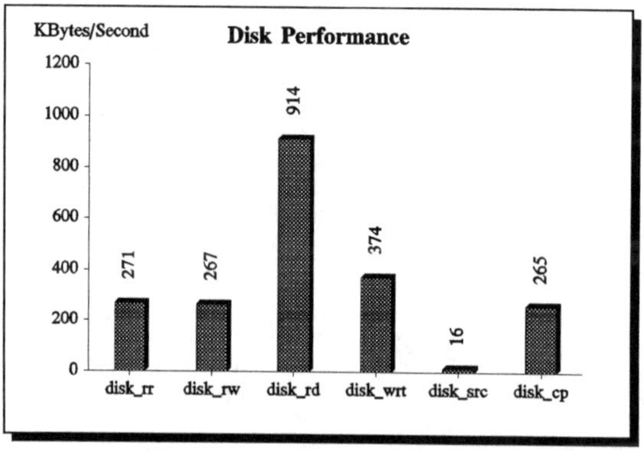

The single-tasking performance of cached disk operations (Random read/ write, Sequential read/write, directory search and copy) is represented in kilobytes per second. Cached disk performance is especially important for interactive applications such as **Software Development and Spreadsheets.**

Independently Certified Performance — AIM TECHNOLOGY — UNIX Systems

Certified By:

AIM Technology

Date: Dec 27, 1993
S/N# 0010

Certified Workstation Report

AIM Technology

A UNIX Performance Summary Based on the AIM Workstation Benchmark and the AIM Independent Resource Benchmark (Release 1.0)

General Workstation Mix

IBM RISC System/6000 POWERstation 230

Price	CPU Type	Clock Rate	1st Level Cache	2nd Level Cache	RAM
N/A	Power 2508	25 MHz	8K	128K	48 MB

Disks	Display	I/O Buffers	O/S	File System	Compiler
1.7 GB, 11.5 ms	1024x768x8 19" Color	Dynamic	AIX v3.2	AIX	xlc v1.2.1

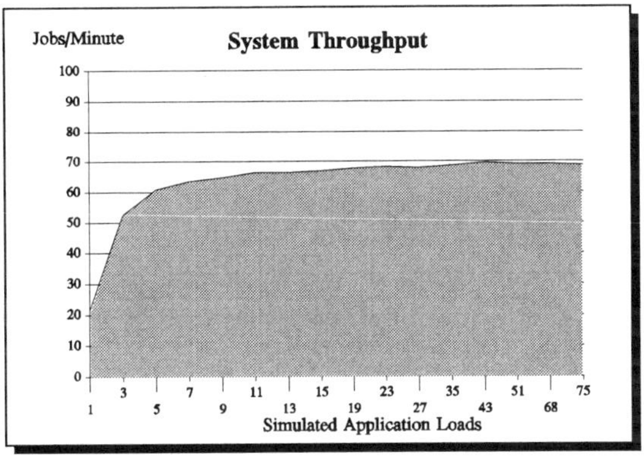

Peak Performance

69.6 AIM Workstation Jobs/Minute

The **Peak Performance** reflects the system throughput at the point at which the system is able to process the most jobs per minute.

Sustained Performance

67.5 AIM Workstation Loads

The **Sustained performance** indicates the multitasking application load where the system's performance could become unacceptable, i.e. less than 1 job/minute/AIM Workstation load.

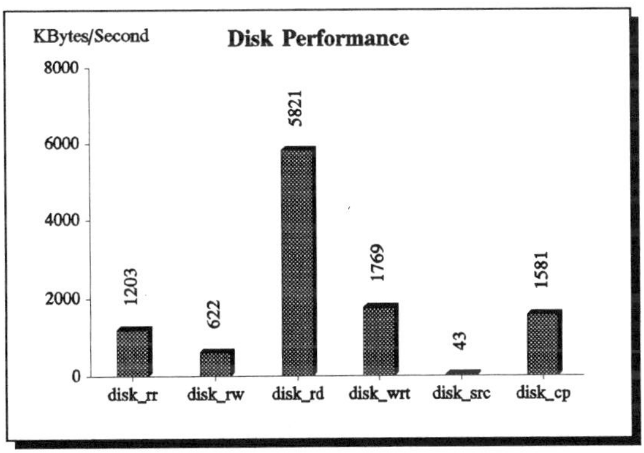

The single-tasking performance of cached disk operations (Random read/ write, Sequential read/write, directory search and copy) is represented in kilobytes per second. Cached disk performance is especially important for interactive applications such as **Software Development and Spreadsheets.**

Certified By:

AIM Technology

Date: Dec 27, 1993

S/N# 0001

Certified Workstation Report

AIM Technology

A UNIX Performance Summary Based on the AIM Workstation Benchmark and the AIM Independent Resource Benchmark (Release 1.0)
Mechanical CAD/Numerical Analysis Mix

IBM RISC System/6000 POWERstation 230

Price	CPU Type	Clock Rate	1st Level Cache	2nd Level Cache	RAM
N/A	Power 2508	25 MHz	8K	128K	48 MB

Disks	Display	I/O Buffers	O/S	File System	Compiler
CASD 2000 1.7 GB, 64 MB Cache	1024x768x8 19" Color	Dynamic	AIX v3.2	AIX	xlc v1.2.1

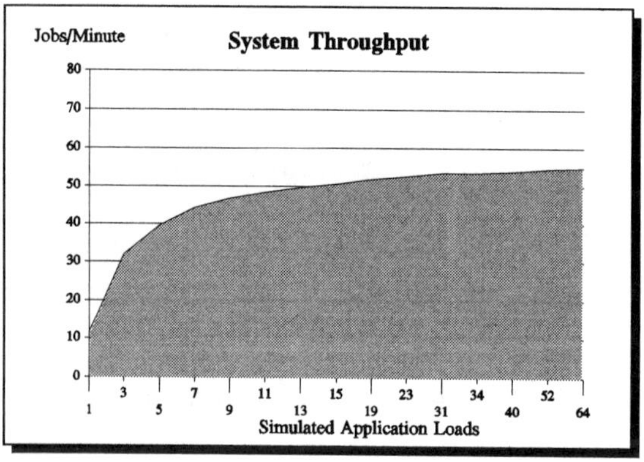

Peak Performance
54.8 AIM MCAD Jobs/Minute

The **Peak Performance** reflects the system throughput at the point at which the system is able to process the most jobs per minute.

Sustained Performance
52.1 AIM MCAD Loads

The **Sustained performance** indicates the multitasking application load where the system's performance could become unacceptable, i.e. less than 1 job/minute/AIM MCAD load.

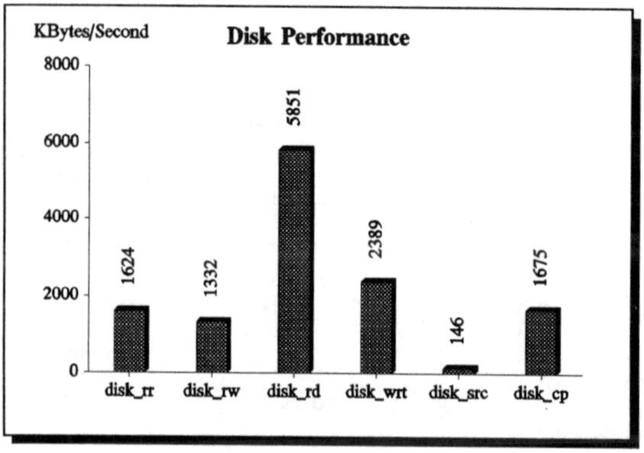

The single-tasking performance of cached disk operations (Random read/ write, Sequential read/write, directory search and copy) is represented in kilobytes per second. Cached disk performance is especially important for interactive applications such as **Software Development and Spreadsheets.**

Certified By:

AIM Technology

Date: Dec 27, 1993
S/N# 0003

Certified Workstation Report

AIM Technology

A UNIX Performance Summary Based on the AIM Workstation Benchmark and the AIM Independent Resource Benchmark (Release 1.0)
GIS/Imaging Mix

IBM RISC System/6000 POWERstation 230

Price	*CPU Type*	*Clock Rate*	*1st Level Cache*	*2nd Level Cache*	*RAM*
N/A	Power 2508	25 MHz	8K	128K	48 MB

Disks	*Display*	*I/O Buffers*	*O/S*	*File System*	*Compiler*
CASD 2000 1.7 GB, 64 MB Cache	1024x768x8 19" Color	Dynamic	AIX v3.2	AIX	xlc v1.2.1

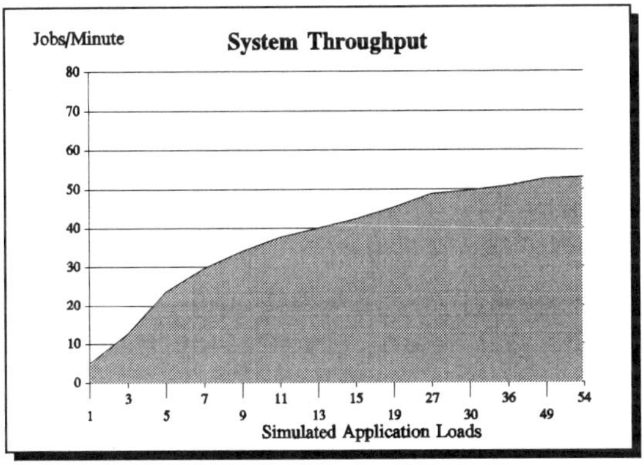

Peak Performance
53 AIM GIS/Imaging Jobs/Minute

The **Peak Performance** reflects the system throughput at the point at which the system is able to process the most jobs per minute.

Sustained Performance
47.8 AIM GIS/Imaging Loads

The **Sustained performance** indicates the multitasking application load where the system's performance could become unacceptable, i.e. less than 1 job/minute/AIM GIS/Imaging load.

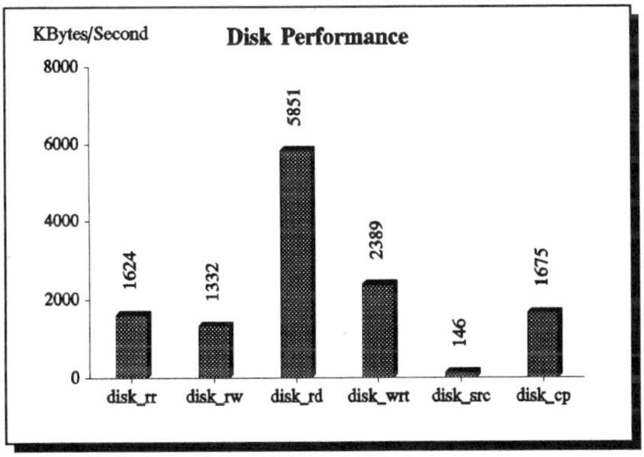

The single-tasking performance of cached disk operations (Random read/ write, Sequential read/write, directory search and copy) is represented in kilobytes per second. Cached disk performance is especially important for interactive applications such as **Software Development and Spreadsheets.**

Certified By:

AIM Technology

Date: Dec 27, 1993
S/N# 0004

Multiuser Performance

The AIM Multiuser Benchmark - Suite VII tests all types of multiuser systems, from compute servers, to file servers, to database servers. The benchmark includes a variety of application mixes that allow AIM and end-users to test any multiuser system in specific types of environments:

- **Multiuser/Shared System Mix**
- **Compute Server Mix**
- **Large Database Mix**
- **File Server Mix**

In addition, AIM and end-users can create custom user mixes to test other application mixes of interest.

The AIM Independent Resource Benchmark - Suite IX measures processing rates for subsystems, I/O transfers, function calls, and UNIX system calls.

The results of these two benchmarks are combined to create Certified Multiuser Reports that detail the performance results for the selected system and application mix. AIM ratings include Peak Performance, Sustained Performance, and the Job Timing Index.

Peak Performance reported in operation jobs per minute, is the system's highest performance level when a significant amount of CPU, floating point, and disk caching is used. Sustained Performance is the measurement taken when the system's capacity is reached; that is, when system performance becomes unacceptable to the user. The Job Timing Index is a measure of the difference in completion times for concurrent jobs, and reveals the ability of a system to run processes simultaneously.

Pages 2 - 4 of each report include performance ratings for Special Interest Areas: disk, floating point, integer math, library routines, system calls, file system, IPC, and algorithmic functions.

Certified Multiuser Report

AIM Technology

A UNIX Performance Summary Based on the AIM Multiuser Benchmark and the AIM Independent Resource Benchmark (Release 1.0)
Compute Server Mix

IBM RISC System/6000 POWERstation 230

Price	*CPU Type*	*Clock Rate*	*1st Level Cache*	*2nd Level Cache*	*RAM*
N/A	Power 2508	25 MHz	8K	128K	48 MB

Disks	*Disk Controllers*	*I/O Buffers*	*O/S*	*File System*	*Compiler*
CASD 2000 1.7 GB, 64 MB Cache	SCSI-II	Dynamic	AIX v3.2	AIX	xlc v1.2.1

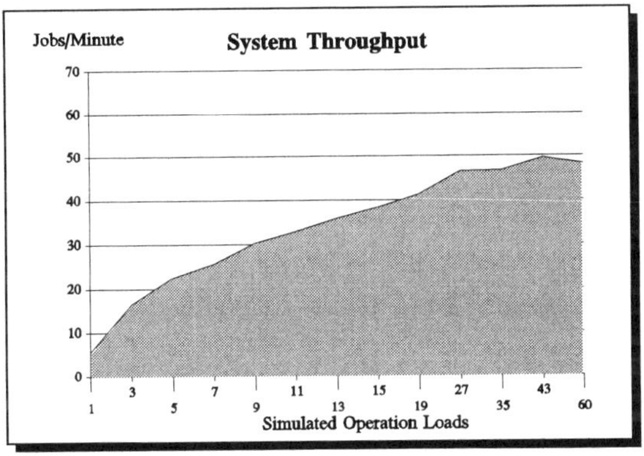

Peak Performance
49.6 AIM Compute Server Jobs/Minute

The **Peak Performance** reflects the system throughput at the point at which the system is able to process the most jobs per minute.

Sustained Performance
44.2 AIM Compute Server Loads

The **Sustained performance** indicates the multitasking operation load where the system's performance could become unacceptable, i.e. less than 1 job/minute/AIM Compute Server load.

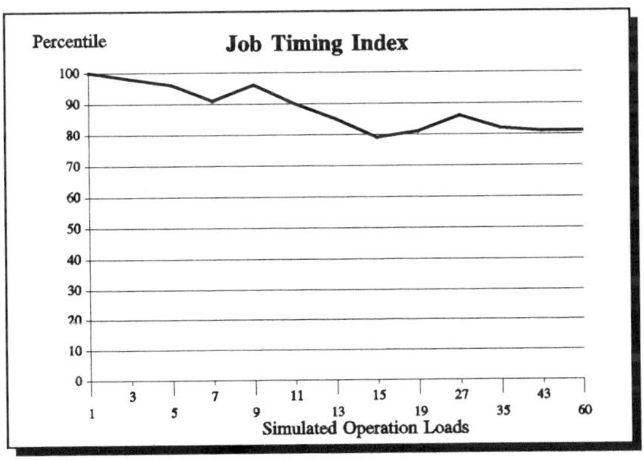

Job Timing Index
79 Percentile

The **Job Timing Index** is a measure of difference in completion times for concurrent jobs. It reveals the ability of a system to run processes simultaneously.

Certified By:

AIM Technology

Date: Dec 28, 1993
S/N# 0005

Certified Multiuser Report

AIM Technology

A UNIX Performance Summary Based on the AIM Multiuser Benchmark and the AIM Independent Resource Benchmark (Release 1.0)
File Server Mix

IBM RISC System/6000 POWERstation 230

Price	*CPU Type*	*Clock Rate*	*1st Level Cache*	*2nd Level Cache*	*RAM*
N/A	Power 2508	25 MHz	8K	128K	48 MB

Disks	*Disk Controllers*	*I/O Buffers*	*O/S*	*File System*	*Compiler*
1.7 GB, 11.5ms	SCSI-II	Dynamic	AIX v3.2	AIX	xlc v1.2.1

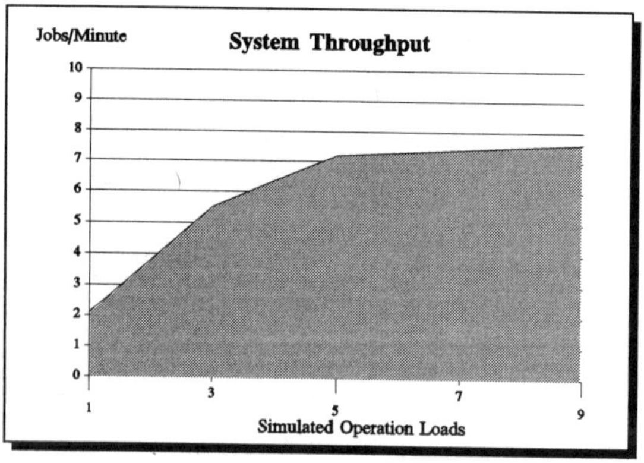

Peak Performance
7.6 AIM File Server Jobs/Minute

The **Peak Performance** reflects the system throughput at the point at which the system is able to process the most jobs per minute.

Sustained Performance
6.2 AIM File Server Loads

The **Sustained performance** indicates the multitasking operation load where the system's performance could become unacceptable, i.e. less than 1 job/minute/AIM File Server load.

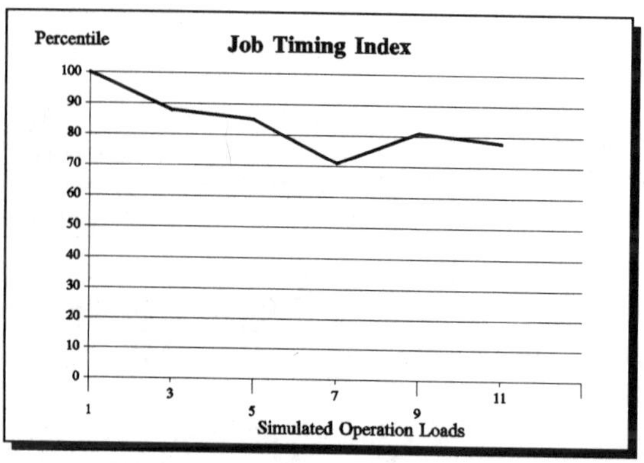

Job Timing Index
71 Percentile

The **Job Timing Index** is a measure of difference in completion times for concurrent jobs. It reveals the ability of a system to run processes simultaneously.

Independently Certified Performance — AIM TECHNOLOGY — UNIX Systems

Certified By:

AIM Technology

Date: Dec 28, 1993
S/N# 0007

Certified Multiuser Report

AIM Technology

A UNIX Performance Summary Based on the AIM Multiuser Benchmark and the AIM Independent Resource Benchmark (Release 1.0)

File Server Mix

Hewlett Packard 9000 Model 715

Price	*CPU Type*	*Clock Rate*	*1st Level Cache*	*2nd Level Cache*	*RAM*
N/A	PA-RISC 7100	33 MHz	8K	128K	48 MB

Disks	*Disk Controllers*	*I/O Buffers*	*O/S*	*File System*	*Compiler*
CASD 2000 1.7 GB, 64 MB Cache	SCSI-II	Dynamic	HPUX 9.01	BFS	cc A.09.16

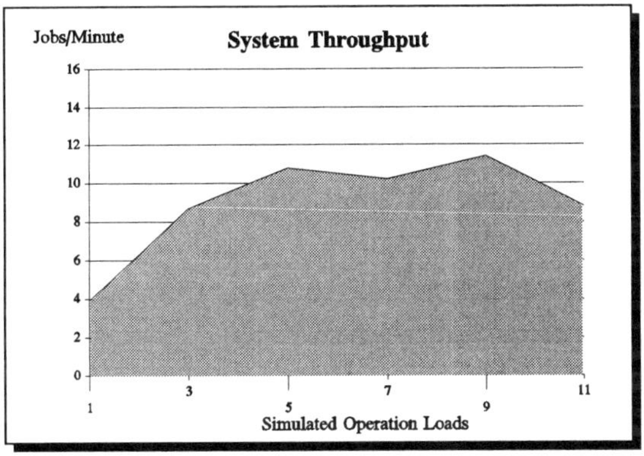

Peak Performance
11.4 AIM File Server Jobs/Minute

The **Peak Performance** reflects the system throughput at the point at which the system is able to process the most jobs per minute.

Sustained Performance
9.4 AIM File Server Loads

The **Sustained performance** indicates the multitasking operation load where the system's performance could become unacceptable, i.e. less than 1 job/minute/AIM File Server load.

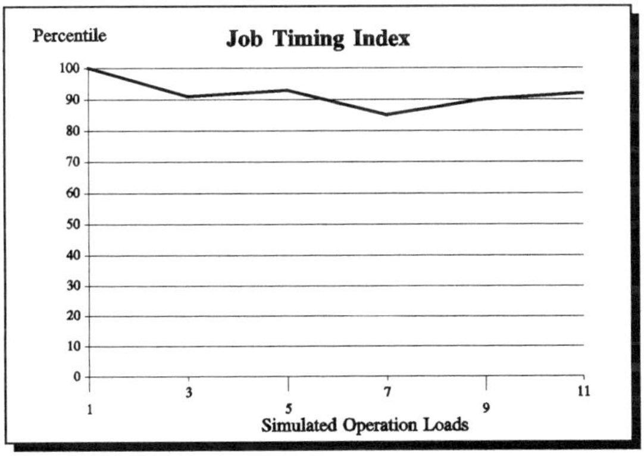

Job Timing Index
85 Percentile

The **Job Timing Index** is a measure of difference in completion times for concurrent jobs. It reveals the ability of a system to run processes simultaneously.

Certified By:

AIM Technology

Date: Dec 28, 1993
S/N# 0008

AIM Technology

Certified Multiuser Report

A UNIX Performance Summary Based on the AIM Multiuser Benchmark and the AIM Independent Resource Benchmark (Release 1.0)

File Server Mix

Hewlett Packard 9000 Model 755

Price	*CPU Type*	*Clock Rate*	*1st Level Cache*	*2nd Level Cache*	*RAM*
N/A	PA-RISC 7100	99 MHz	8K	128K	64 MB

Disks	*Disk Controllers*	*I/O Buffers*	*O/S*	*File System*	*Compiler*
1.0 GB, 10.5ms	SCSI-II	Dynamic	HPUX 9.01	HPUX	HPUX CC

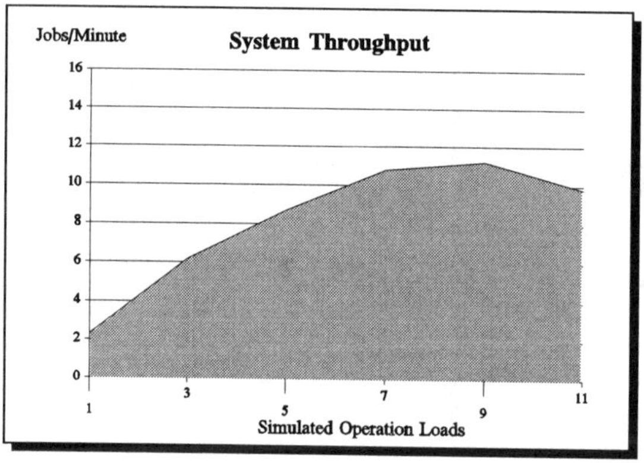

Peak Performance

11.2 AIM File Server Jobs/Minute

The **Peak Performance** reflects the system throughput at the point at which the system is able to process the most jobs per minute.

Sustained Performance

8.9 AIM File Server Loads

The **Sustained performance** indicates the multitasking operation load where the system's performance could become unacceptable, i.e. less than 1 job/minute/AIM File Server load.

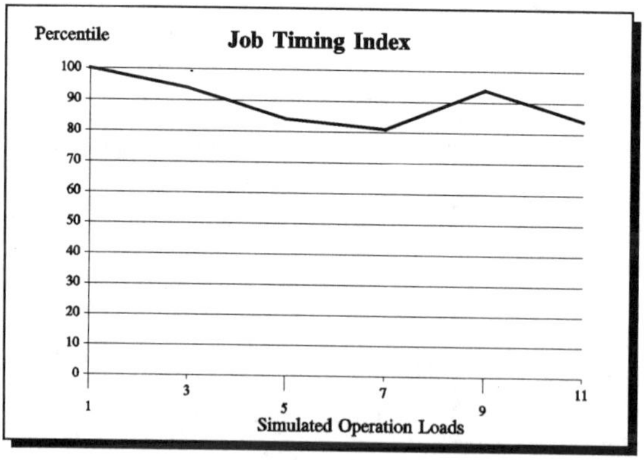

Job Timing Index

81 Percentile

The **Job Timing Index** is a measure of difference in completion times for concurrent jobs. It reveals the ability of a system to run processes simultaneously.

Certified By:

AIM Technology

Date: Dec 28, 1993
S/N# 0013

Certified Multiuser Report

AIM Technology

A UNIX Performance Summary Based on the AIM Multiuser Benchmark and the AIM Independent Resource Benchmark (Release 1.0)

File Server Mix

SUN SPARCserver 670

Price	*CPU Type*	*Clock Rate*	*1st Level Cache*	*2nd Level Cache*	*RAM*
N/A	SPARC	40 MHz	None	1 MB	64 MB

Disks	*Disk Controllers*	*I/O Buffers*	*O/S*	*File System*	*Compiler*
1.0 GB, 10.5ms	SCSI-II	Dynamic	Solaris 2.2	UFS	GNU C

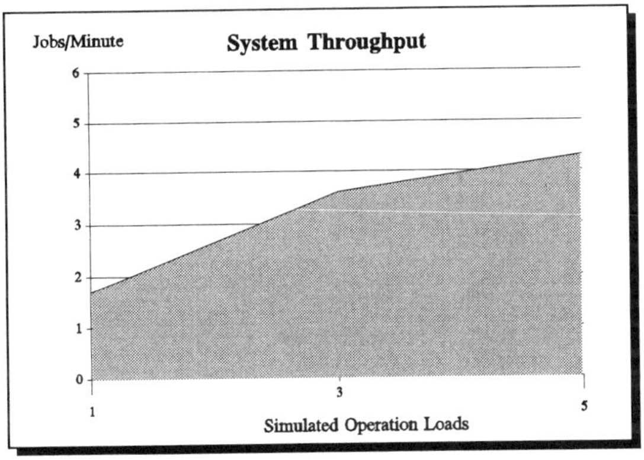

Peak Performance
4.3 AIM File Server Jobs/Minute

The **Peak Performance** reflects the system throughput at the point at which the system is able to process the most jobs per minute.

Sustained Performance
3.0 AIM File Server Loads

The **Sustained performance** indicates the multitasking operation load where the system's performance could become unacceptable, i.e. less than 1 job/minute/AIM File Server load.

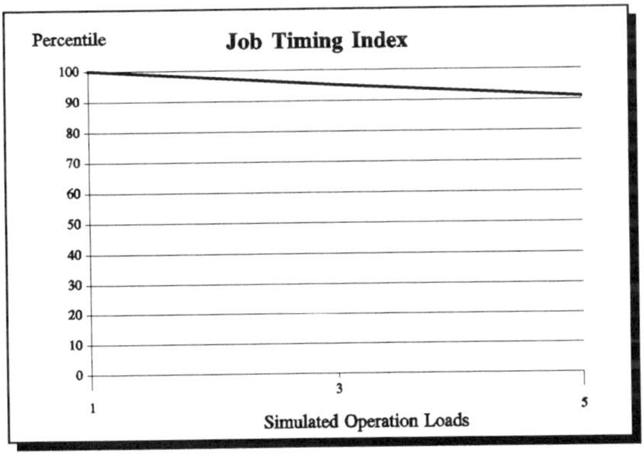

Job Timing Index
91 Percentile

The **Job Timing Index** is a measure of difference in completion times for concurrent jobs. It reveals the ability of a system to run processes simultaneously.

Certified By:

AIM Technology

Date: Dec 28, 1993
S/N# 0011

Certified Multiuser Report

AIM Technology

A UNIX Performance Summary Based on the AIM Multiuser Benchmark and the AIM Independent Resource Benchmark (Release 1.0)

Shared Model Mix

IBM RISC System/6000 POWERstation 230

Price	*CPU Type*	*Clock Rate*	*1st Level Cache*	*2nd Level Cache*	*RAM*
N/A	Power 2508	25 MHz	8K	128K	48 MB

Disks	*Disk Controllers*	*I/O Buffers*	*O/S*	*File System*	*Compiler*
1.7 GB, 11.5ms	SCSI-II	Dynamic	AIX v3.2	AIX	xlc v1.2.1

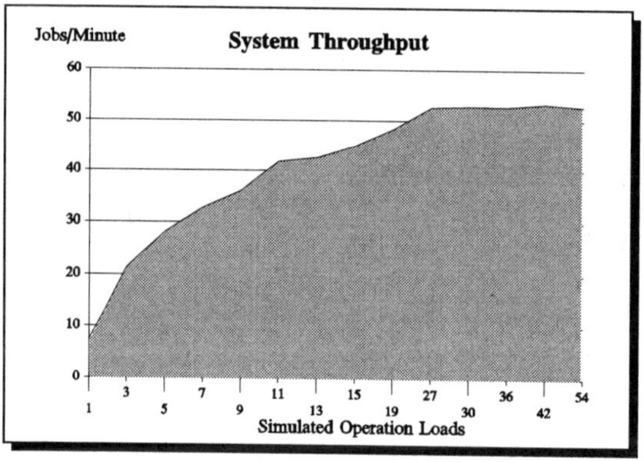

Peak Performance
53.3 AIM Multiuser Jobs/Minute

The **Peak Performance** reflects the system throughput at the point at which the system is able to process the most jobs per minute.

Sustained Performance
49.2 AIM Multiuser Loads

The **Sustained performance** indicates the multitasking operation load where the system's performance could become unacceptable, i.e. less than 1 job/minute/AIM Multiuser load.

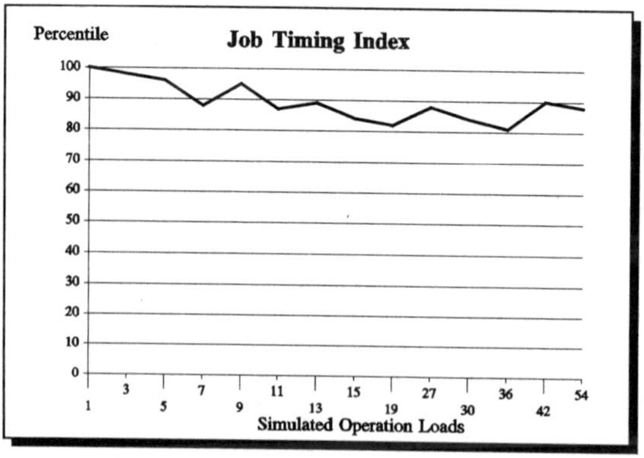

Job Timing Index
81 Percentile

The **Job Timing Index** is a measure of difference in completion times for concurrent jobs. It reveals the ability of a system to run processes simultaneously.

Certified By:

AIM Technology

Date: Dec 28, 1993
S/N# 0006

X Windows Performance

This section presents AIM-certified X Windows performance results for a variety of X terminals and workstations. Each report includes an overall rating, as well as ratings for the following major application environments and functional areas:

- Engineering (for example, CAD/CAM, CAE and other graphics intensive applications)
- Desktop Publishing (rapid display of volumes of variable font textual data, with some graphics displays interspersed in the text)
- Software Development (fixed font text and window operations)
- Drawing (lines, polygons, circles, etc.)
- Text (including fixed and variable fonts)
- Pixmaps (including icon sized and larger)
- Windows (creating, deleting, and circulating)

In all cases, the higher the rating, the better the performance.

Suite X is designed to run in a variety of environments and fit on most currently used X display devices.

Complete performance reports for all of the systems that appear in this guide are available from AIM Technology. In addition to the information displayed in this section, the complete reports include detailed results of 115 separate X tests.

AIM X Windows Performance Report

An X Windows Performance Summary Based on the AIM Suite X Benchmark

Hewlett-Packard 9000 Model 715/33

AIM X Rating

7.6 AIM/X's

The **AIM X Windows Rating** reflects the overall X Windows performance of this system. A NCD19 X Terminal typically rates 1 AIM/X.

Host System

Price	*N/A*
Cpu Type	*PA-RISC 7100*
Clock Rate	*33 MHz*
Ext. Cpu Cache	*128 KB*
Floating Point	*Integrated*
RAM	*48 MB*
Disk 1	*1.7 GB, 3ms*
Disk 2	
Disk Controllers	*SCSI*
I/O Buffers	*Dynamic*
O/S	*HP-UX 9.01*
Compiler	*HP C A.09.19*
X Software	*HP VUE 3.0* *X11R5*

Display Server

Price	*N/A*
Display	*19" Color*
Resolution	*1280x1024*
Bit Planes	*8*
Refresh Rate	*60 Hz*
Processor	*N/A*
Coprocessor	*N/A*
Local Memory	*N/A*
Local Disk	*N/A*
X Software	*N/A*

Network

Ethernet LAN w/ TCP/IP

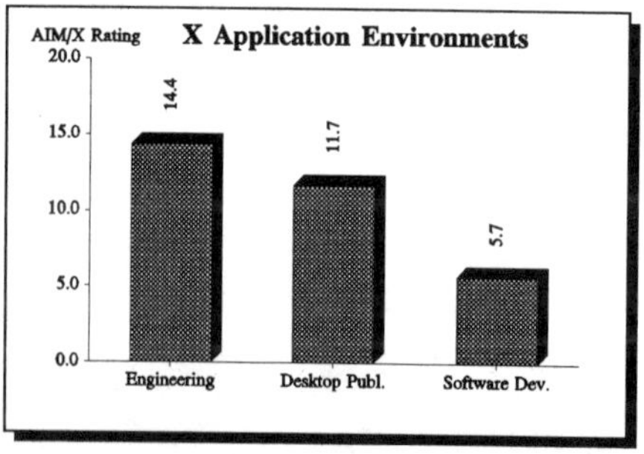

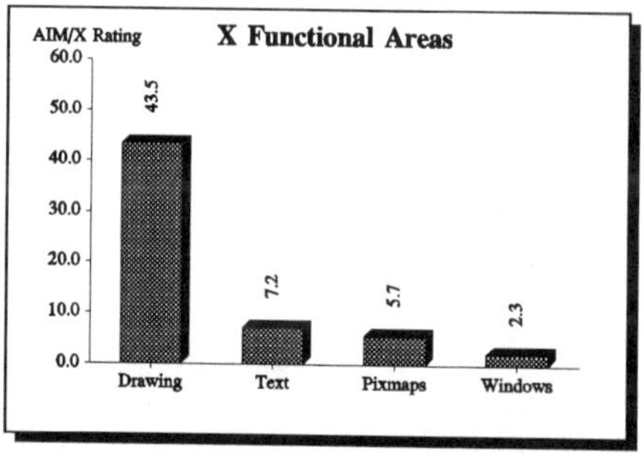

Performance Ratings for Engineering (CAD/CAM/CAE), Desktop Publishing, and Software Development environments are indicated above. Ratings are relative to AIM/X Ratings for a NCD19 X Terminal.

Performance Ratings for Drawing (lines and curves), Text, Pixmap (background graphics operations), and Window operations are indicated above. Ratings are relative to AIM/X Ratings for a NCD19 X Terminal.

AIM X Windows Performance Report

An X Windows Performance Summary Based on the AIM Suite X Benchmark

IBM RISC System/6000 POWERstation 230

AIM X Rating

8.0 AIM/X's

The **AIM X Windows Rating** reflects the overall X Windows performance of this system. A NCD19 X Terminal typically rates 1 AIM/X.

Host System

Price	*N/A*
Cpu Type	*POWER 3364*
Clock Rate	*33 MHz*
Ext. Cpu Cache	*128 KB*
Floating Point	*Integrated*
RAM	*48 MB*
Disk 1	*1 GB, 11.5ms*
Disk 2	
Disk Controllers	*SCSI*
I/O Buffers	*Dynamic*
O/S	*AIX v3.2*
Compiler	*xlc*
X Software	*AIXwindows 1.2.3 X11R5*

Display Server

Price	*N/A*
Display	*16" Color*
Resolution	*1280x1024*
Bit Planes	*8*
Refresh Rate	*72 HZ*
Processor	*N/A*
Coprocessor	*N/A*
Local Memory	*N/A*
Local Disk	*N/A*
X Software	*N/A*

Network

Ethernet LAN w/ TCP/IP

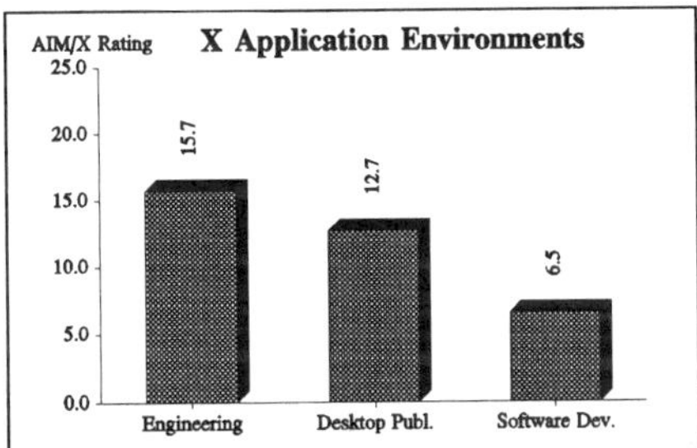

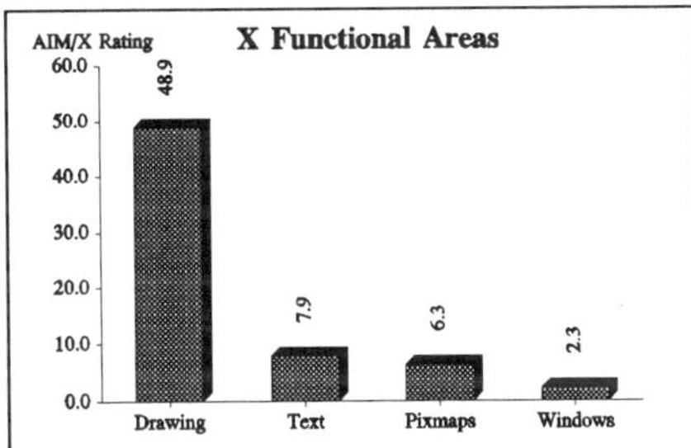

Performance Ratings for Engineering (CAD/CAM/CAE), Desktop Publishing, and Software Development environments are indicated above. Ratings are relative to AIM/X Ratings for a NCD19 X Terminal.

Performance Ratings for Drawing (lines and curves), Text, Pixmap (background graphics operations), and Window operations are indicated above. Ratings are relative to AIM/X Ratings for a NCD19 X Terminal.

AIM X Windows Performance Report

An X Windows Performance Summary Based on the AIM Suite X Benchmark

Sun SPARCstation IPC

AIM X Rating

3.1 AIM/X's

The **AIM X Windows Rating** reflects the overall X Windows performance of this system. A NCD19 X Terminal typically rates 1 AIM/X.

Host System

Price	*$7,295*
Cpu Type	*SPARC*
Clock Rate	*25 MHz*
Ext. Cpu Cache	*64 KB*
Floating Point	*SPARC*
RAM	*24 MB*
Disk 1	*207 MB*
Disk 2	N/A
Disk Controllers	*SUN SCSI*
I/O Buffers	*Dynamic*
O/S	*SUN OS 4.1.2*
Compiler	*SUN cc*
X Software	*OpenWindows 2.0*

Display Server

Price	*N/A*
Display	*16" Color*
Resolution	*1152x900*
Bit Planes	*8*
Refresh Rate	*66 Hz, non-interlaced*
Processor	*N/A*
Coprocessor	*(none)*
Local Memory	*N/A*
Local Disk	*N/A*
X Software	*N/A*

Network

ThinNet Ethernet

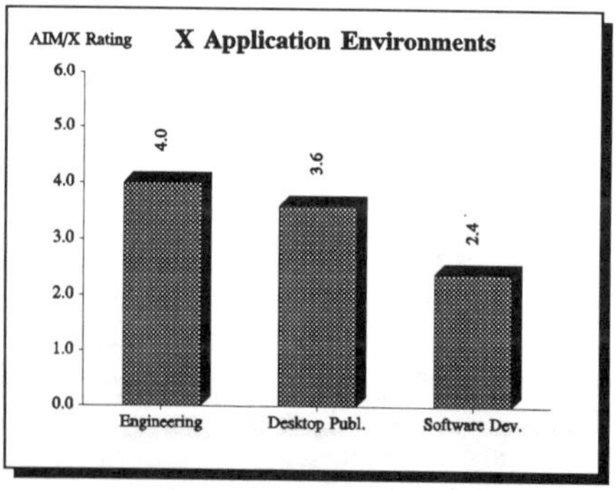

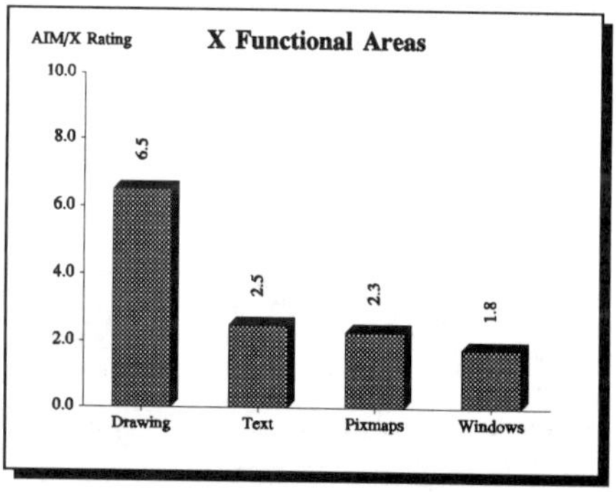

Performance Ratings for Engineering (CAD/CAM/CAE), Desktop Publishing, and Software Development environments are indicated above. Ratings are relative to AIM/X Ratings for a NCD19 X Terminal.

Performance Ratings for Drawing (lines and curves), Text, Pixmap (background graphics operations), and Window operations are indicated above. Ratings are relative to AIM/X Ratings for a NCD19 X Terminal.

The AIM Independent Resource Benchmark - Suite IX

The AIM Independent Resource Benchmark™ exercises and times each component of a UNIX™ computer system, independently. Unlike other benchmarks that calculate a system-level measurement of system performance, this benchmark yields specific results on a per-test basis.

Benchmark Tests

The benchmark uses 58 subtests to generate absolute processing rates, in operations per second, for subsystems, I/O transfers, function calls, and UNIX system calls.

Each test repeats an operation, system call, or I/O transfer for a specified time (user specifies test run time).

In addition, you can add a custom test by supplying C code or modifying the benchmark's shell scripts.

System Requirements

This benchmark will compile and run on most POSIX-compliant UNIX systems. All source code is in ANSI C. To assure its portability, the program uses standard system calls.

Benchmark Reports

The benchmark generates a tab delimited spreadsheet output file that contains data for the following parameters:

- Arithmetic
- InterProcess Communication
- Disk/Filesystem I/O
- Library/System
- Memory and Process Management
- Function Calls
- Algorithmic Tests

You can use this data to produce a PostScript output file.

Benchmark Results

Benchmark results can be used to:

- Compare different machines on a test-by-test basis.
- Make changes to system configuration and rerun to see effect.
- Make changes to compiler and load options and rerun to see effect.
- Measure the success or failure of system tuning and configuration changes on a single system.
- Use the benchmark results to set an absolute maximum performance level for each system resource. This is possible because resources are tested individually.
- Identify strengths and weaknesses of a system.
- Use as a guide to optimization/configuration plans. For example, if IPC results show a wide variance between methods, consider configuring the system to use the method that is giving the higher performance level.

Certified Multiuser and Workstation Reports

AIM combines the results from this benchmark with the results of the Workstation Benchmark and Multiuser Benchmark to generate a Certified Workstation Report and Certified Multiuser Report, respectively.

These reports identify Peak and Sustained ratings as well as ratings for other system functions.

After Market Spotlight: Zitel CASD Disk Add-on

See Related Article "Improving File Performance" on Page 9

	SUN SPARC server 670 Before	SUN SPARC server 670 After	Hewlett Packard 9000 Model 755 Before	Hewlett Packard 9000 Model 755 After
Peak Performance	4.3	13.7	11.2	29.4
Sustained Performance	3.0	9.8	8.9	22
Job Timing Index	91	86	81	90
CPU Type	SPARC	SPARC`	PA-RISC 7100	PA-RISC 7100
Clock Rate	40 MHz	40 MHz	99 MHz	99 MHz
1st Level Cache	None	None	8K	8K
2nd Level Cache	1 MB	1 MB	128K	128K
RAM	64 MB	64 MB	64 MB	64 MB
Disks	1.0 GB, 10.5ms	CASD 2000 2.0 GB, 64 MB Cache	1.0 GB, 10.5ms	CASD 2000 2.0 GB, 64 MB Cache
Disk Controllers	SCSI-II	SCSI-II	SCSI-II	SCSI-II
I/O Buffers	Dynamic	Dynamic	Dynamic	Dynamic
O/S	Solaris 2.2	Solaris 2.2	HPUX 9.01	HPUX 9.01
File System	UFS	UFS	HPUX	HPUX
Compiler	GNU C	GNU C	HPUX CC	HPUX CC

SCO UNIX Performance

Top performers in peak performance and sustained performance.

System	AIMs	User Loads
Acer Altos 700	25.9	141
Acer Altos 7000 (486DX2)	26.9	225
Acer Altos 7000 (Pentium)	38.8	290
Acer Altos 17000	50.7	343
Altos System 15000 (1 CPU)	27.8	255
Altos System 15000 (2 CPU)	51.8	379
Altos System 15000 (4 CPU)	86.4	565
AST Manhattan SMP	53.3	454
AST Manhattan SMP (2 CPU)	81.9	723
AST Manhattan SMP (4 CPU)	114.1	998
Compaq ProLiant 1000 4/66 Model 2100A	29.1	284
Compaq ProLiant 1000 5/60 Model 2100A	44.4	406
Compaq ProLiant 2000 5/66 Model 2100A	104.4	998
COMPAQ ProSignia	30.2	222
Compaq SYSTEMPRO/XL (486)	54.4	529
Compaq SYSTEMPRO/XL (Pentium)	103.1	976
DEC applicationDEC 400XP	27.7	230
DECpc 450ST	27.7	230
ICL FX486/33	14.4	135
Tricord ES5000	125.7	1078
Zenith Data Systems Z-Server EX P60E Model 1000A	50.7	429
Zenith Z-Server 450DE Model 500	28.8	237
Zenith Z-Server LT P60E Model 500	50.7	382

RFPs: Preparing Specifications for Procurements

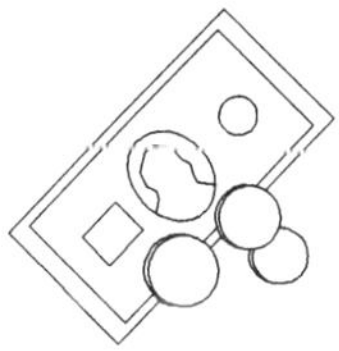

Why performance data?

The availability of compatible Open Systems from a wide range of vendors has increased the need for users to require performance data as part of their procurement process. The procurement process, similar to individual buying decisions, requires that the performance criteria used for selection and/or purchase be documented in a specification.

How can I get the results?

Data from AIM Performance Reports and/or AIM benchmark results can be used as criteria in specifications. For example, if a specification requires peak performance, you can require that all systems meet or exceed 50 AIMs (a unit of peak performance reported extensively in this guide). When you require prospective bidders to obtain AIM performance results for specific machine configurations, you can ensure that the proposed systems meet your minimum requirements.

Weighing bidders' responses

Evaluate the performance results that you receive from each bidder to determine if their bid meets your requirements. You can also award additional evaluation points when performance is exceeded without an increase in cost.

Sample specifications

The following paragraphs include a variety of sample specifications. Each sample specification recommends how to prepare your written request for bids so that your system requirements will be met and bidders will submit uniform responses.

Checking it over

More than one example may apply to your system requirements. More detailed specifications can be developed by requesting a copy of AIM's free booklet, Sample Performance Specifications for UNIX Systems. Use this information to understand selection criteria and to streamline the buying/procurement process. If you want to verify the accuracy of your performance requirements before publishing your RFP, or if you need assistance, AIM Technology will provide additional information or help adapt these examples to your specific needs.

Sample Performance Specifications

<u>*REQUIREMENT*</u>
Identify bidder's relative UNIX system performance.

Objective - The text below describes how to obtain independent third party performance reports to evaluate relative system performance. Report parameters can be used for workstation, compute server, file server, or multiuser system capability.

Sample Text - Each vendor must submit a copy of the AIM Performance Report for the proposed system with their bid. Please ensure that the report is for the exact system configuration submitted for the bid. You may contact AIM Technology at (800) 848-8649 or in CA, at (408) 748-8649.

<u>*REQUIREMENT*</u>
Limit response to systems with minimum performance levels.

Objective - The text below describes how to obtain independent third party performance reports that validate minimum performance levels. Report parameters can be used for workstation, compute server, file server, or multiuser system capability.

Sample Text - Each vendor must submit a copy of the AIM Performance Report for the proposed system with their bid. To qualify, the proposed system must provide a minimum AIM Performance Rating of 50 AIMs and a Maximum User Load Rating of at least 400 User Loads. Please ensure that the report is for the exact system configuration submitted for the bid. You may contact AIM Technology at (800) 848-8649 or in CA, at (408) 748-8649.

<u>*REQUIREMENT*</u>
Identify relative performance for user-specified application workloads.

Objective - The text below describes how to obtain independent third party performance for specific applications.

Sample Text - Each vendor must submit a copy of the AIM Application Performance Report for the proposed system with their bid. The following application model must be used: 75% db (data base), and 25% wp (word processing). Please ensure that the report is for the exact system configuration submitted for the bid. You may contact AIM Technology at (800) 848-8649 or in CA, at (408) 748-8649.

REQUIREMENT
Determine relative X Windows workstation or X Terminal performance.

Objective - The text below describes how to specify X Windows performance requirements.

Sample Text - Each vendor must submit a copy of the AIM Performance Report - X for the proposed system with their bid. Please ensure that the report is for the exact system configuration submitted for the bid. You may contact AIM Technology at (800) 848-8649 or in CA, at (408) 748-8649.

REQUIREMENT
Identify relative workstation performance with network server.

Objective - The text below describes how to customize your requirements to obtain information on this important aspect of network performance.

Sample Text - Each vendor must submit a copy of the AIM Application Performance Report - Workstation for the proposed system with their bid. The following configuration options must be used: Virtual Memory Exerciser ON, Line Printer test ON, TTY I/O test ON at 1200 baud, and 8 disk directories specified, 6 local and 2 remote mounted to a file server via Ethernet with TCP/IP (server system to be specified). Please ensure that the report is for the exact system configuration submitted for the bid. You may contact AIM Technology at (800) 848-8649 or in CA, at (408) 748-8649.

A Sample Specification: Oregon Liquor Control Commission

The following details are extracted from a specification prepared by John S. Espy, System Manager, of the Oregon Liquor Control Commission. This example shows how you can include an AIM Performance Report as a requirement in a specification to help you identify the systems that meet your performance criteria. (A series of three dots (...) indicates that, due to space constraints, text has been omitted.)

...Vendors may submit a copy of the AIM Performance Report II for the proposed system with their bid. Please ensure that the report is for the exact system configuration submitted for the bid. You may contact AIM Technology at (800) 848-8649 or in California, at (408) 748-8649.

AIM Reports for other than the exact configuration bid may be submitted as long as they are for the same make, model and configuration of the CPU and operating system as the system proposed. However, points will be deducted for variations in memory, disk size and models, controllers, and other pertinent features...

Points will be awarded as follows: 1000 points will be awarded to the vendor with the highest AIM Performance Rating. Lesser points will be awarded to other vendors based upon the ratio to their AIM Performance Rating to that of the highest performer. For example, if the highest performance rating is 59.4 AIMs, the vendor with this rating will receive 1000 points and a vendor with 29.7 AIMs will receive 500 points. Points for variations of the proposed configuration from the reported configuration will be deducted after the above calculation of points. Therefore, it is possible that no vendor will receive 1000 points if the highest performing machine is not for the exact configuration proposed.

WEIGHTING OF DESIRABLES: (3075 points)

Feature	Points Possible
a. OPEN SYSTEMS (250) 1. Compliance with "open systems" standards	250
b. HARDWARE (650) 1. Symmetric multiprocessing...	100...
c. SOFTWARE (850) 1. Expand file system beyond 2GB...	50...
d. INSTALLATION (0) No desirables	0
e. SUPPORT (100) 1. Quality of hardware maintenance 2. Quality of software maintenance and training	50 50
f. REFERENCES (75) 1. Reference accounts responses 2. User group publication	50 25
g. SYSTEM PERFORMANCE (1000) 1. AIM Technology Performance Rating	1000

AIM Benchmark Products and Services

Since 1982, AIM Technology has set industry standards in performance measurement. The Load/Mix Modeling style of benchmarking, a proprietary technique pioneered by AIM, accurately simulates both the resource loading and the application instruction mix of a user's environment. These features enable AIM's system benchmarks to provide extremely accurate results with little effort on the part of the user.

AIM's newest products and services include the **AIM Workstation Benchmark - Suite VI**, **AIM Multiuser Benchmark - Suite VII**, **AIM Independent Resource Benchmark - Suite IX**, and the **Certified Workstation Report (CWR)** and **Certified Multiuser Report (CMR)**. AIM continues to feature the **AIM Performance Report Certification Service** as well as a complete line of accurate system and subsystem benchmarks: the **AIM System Benchmark - Suite III**, the **AIM UNIX Utilities Benchmark - Milestone**, the **AIM X Windows Benchmark - Suite X**, and the **AIM Subsystem Benchmark - Suite II**.

The following pages briefly describe the newest products and services as well as the Performance Report Certification Service and each of the AIM benchmarks. For more information about any of these products, call AIM Technology at (800) 848-8649 (outside California) or (408) 748-8649.

AIM Certification Services

AIM Certified Reports

AIM offers the AIM Certification Services, a third party system evaluation and publishing service that consists of a system performance evaluation by AIM personnel, and the production of a summary report with both system and component level results in an easy to read format.

AIM Certification Reports are typically used in bids for RFP responses, for internal system evaluations and tuning, for competitive positioning, and as sales tools. Reports are published and distributed by AIM to thousands of UNIX computer buyers and system manufacturers in AIM's **UNIX System Price/Performance Guide** and **AIM's Performance Report Series**. Reports are also distributed at trade shows and to the press. AIM's database of published reports is often consulted by computer buyers to establish performance criteria.

The newest certified reports are the **Certified Workstation Report** and the **Certified Multiuser Report**. AIM uses the AIM Workstation Benchmark - Suite VI results along with the AIM Independent Resource Benchmark - Suite IX to generate the Certified Workstation Reports, and the AIM Multiuser Benchmark - Suite VII and the AIM Independent Resource Benchmark - Suite IX results to generate the Certified Multiuser Reports. These reports detail the performance results for the selected system and application mix.

The Certified Workstation Report displays a system throughput graph which illustrates the system's performance at various application loads. The report also includes the system's two ratings: Peak Performance in application jobs per minute (the system's highest performance level when a significant amount of CPU, floating point, and disk caching is used) and Sustained Performance (the measurement taken when the system's capacity is reached, that is, when system performance becomes unacceptable to the user).

The Certified Multiuser Report also includes a System Throughput Graph which shows the system's performance at various operation loads as well as the Peak and Sustained Performance ratings described above.

AIM also produces the **AIM Performance Report** and the **AIM Performance Report - X**. These Performance Reports feature certified multitasking system performance results as well as individual subsystem performance information. In addition, the AIM Performance Report - X shows comprehensive X Windows performance results.

AIM certified reports and benchmarks are used extensively by commercial and government industries to justify computer systems for procurement, and by nearly all major computer manufacturers worldwide.

AIM Benchmarks

Workstation Benchmark - Suite VI

Workstations are used by all types of people for many different reasons. Uses include general business, accounting, software development, and design work to name just a few. AIM Technology took this diversity into consideration when we created our new workstation benchmark. Modeled for a variety of applications, the Workstation Benchmark tests the performance of a system based on the applications that will run on the system.

With AIM's Load Mix Modeling you are able to construct a mix of tests for the intended applications. AIM has developed four standard mixes for the workstation benchmark. If the system is heavily used for General Workstation, Mechanical CAD/Numeric Analysis, GIS/Imaging, or General Business, you can test the system's performance with the standard mixes. If you have a more customized application mix, you can evaluate which tests require emphasis and AIM will create a new mix specifically for your needs.

- The **General Workstation Mix** models software development, digital design, and technical publication environments. These types of application environments place similar stress on workstations.
- The **Mechanical CAD/Numeric Analysis Mix** models 3D, thermal analysis, and astrophysics application environments.
- The **GIS/Imaging Mix** was created to test systems used in environments that require multimedia and graphically intense systems.
- The **General Business Mix** was designed for the "typical" user that loads an application, searches for a file, and uses sophisticated tools such as spreadsheet programs, word processing, presentations, etc.
- **Custom User Mixes** can be created for user's whose environments are not represented by our standard mixes. You can create your own custom user mix or ask AIM's Customer Support staff for assistance. A custom user mix can be created by:
  - Varying the standard mix to more closely model the applications that will run on the system under test
  - Adding C language tests
  - Adding shell scripts

Multiuser Benchmark - Suite VII

Multiuser systems are used in a wide variety of work environments. The AIM multiuser benchmark was designed to test the performance of compute servers, file servers, and multiuser systems that are used primarily to maintain databases. This benchmark runs on the most advanced systems and tests features required by modern Open Systems multiuser environments.

AIM uses Load Mix Modeling to test how well multiuser systems perform under different application loads. The benchmark includes four standard mixes of tests that cover the "standard" uses of large computer systems. If the system is heavily used as a compute server, file server, or to maintain databases, you can use one of the standard mixes to test the system: Multiuser/ Shared System, Compute Server, Large Database, and File Server.

- The **Multiuser/Shared System Mix** models a multiuser environment emphasizing office automation; word processing, spreadsheet, email, database, payroll, and data processing. This mix represents a broad use of different applications, as opposed to a great deal of emphasis on one type of application.
- The **Compute Server Mix** models compute intense environments. This mix is representative of a system that takes on a big "job" or problem, stores it in memory, and hammers away until the "answer" or solution is verified.

- The **Large Database Mix** models systems with very large databases that are constantly updated.
- The **File Server Mix** models many integer compute file system operations in heavy concentration.

Independent Resource Benchmark - Suite IX

There are many different components to a computer system. AIM benchmarks are designed to test the overall performance of a computer system. With so many different components to a system, many benchmarks test the system as a whole as opposed to narrowing in on the specific areas of importance. With AIM's Independent Resource Benchmark-Suite IX, each component is tested independently. There are tests for disk, floating point, integer, operating system, file system, and library to name a few. Each of theses components are exercised and timed, producing their performance results.

This benchmark can be used in conjunction with AIM's Workstation Benchmark - Suite VI or with AIM's Multiuser Benchmark - Suite VII. If used with AIM benchmarks, you can understand the performance of the system as a whole as well as each area of importance and how it affects the overall performance of the system.

System Benchmark - Suite III

UNIX systems typically consist of a centralized multiuser system or file server that supports many users at terminals or workstations. To find the user load level that will exceed the system's capacity, the **System Benchmark (Suite III)** adds simulated user loads and applications to the system, and continues until it reaches a pre-defined number, or until the system stops accepting new loads. **Suite III** allows users to

- Select a range of simulated users.
- Define application environments (for example, 80% database, 20% word processing).
- Define system resources such as terminals (TTY) and printers.
- Customize the benchmark by adding functional tests.
- Plan for future computing requirements (capacity planning).

Suite III performs the following tasks:

- Measures the multiuser system performance of multiple systems under a variety of application mixes and resource loads.
- Compares the multiuser performance of up to 20 single or multiprocessor systems at a time.
- Predicts the effects of adding users to a system under a given application mix and resource load.
- Uses 31 functional tests to evaluate system performance under

user-defined application models.

- Simulates Accounting, Compiling, Data Base, Scientific, Spreadsheet, Word Processing, or other user-defined tasks.

Suite III includes the following reporting facilities:

- Reports that show how long it takes a user to complete a specific number of tasks while additional users, performing similar tasks, are added to the system.
- A report generator that offers two performance reports: the Multiuser Response Time Report includes test time in seconds for each workload level, and the User Throughput Report includes processes per second for each user level.

UNIX Utilities Benchmark - Milestone

Buyers need to know how a system will perform under normal operating conditions. These conditions include disk, terminal, and other peripheral input/output. A truly useful benchmark reflects most, if not all, of the characteristics of an actual user workload. Like AIM's other benchmark products, the **UNIX Utilities Benchmark (Milestone)** simulates real-life conditions and produces meaningful results.

Milestone simulates a pre-defined mix of user types (Administrative Assistant, Calculator/Spreadsheet User, Database User, Manager, Scientist, Software Engineer, and Text Processing User) performing day to day tasks at normal user load levels. **Milestone** uses standard editing, compilation, and typesetting facilities, among others, to exercise the CPU, disk, terminals, and printer. **Milestone** then produces a report that displays the elapsed time and load average for each simulated user load level. **The elapsed time shows you the speed of the system. The load average tells you how well the system handles multiprocessing and contention for I/O devices and, to a lesser degree, the speed of the system.**

Key features of **Milestone**:

- Extremely portable and results are highly repeatable.
- Good real-life quality. **Milestone** uses actual UNIX tools, is functionally representative of real user loads, and is immune to excessive instruction and data caching caused by locality of reference.
- Allows the use of terminal and/or windows and/or LAN terminal lines for output.
- Supports use of user-defined intra-command and inter-command think time delays, and three types of think times: long, normal, and short.
- Transparent to its execution environment. This makes it ideal for use on diskless workstations and multiprocessor systems.
- Reports system performance for one to seven simultaneous user loads and generates a performance rating, the Milestone Index.

X Windows Benchmark - Suite X

Suite X offers both detailed and summary analysis of X Windows based system and server performance. To make test results easy to understand, **Suite X** summarizes the results into effectiveness ratings in four X operation categories (graphics, text, pixmaps, and windows) and three primary X user environments (engineering, desktop publishing, and software development).

Suite X provides 115 specific tests that measure performance in each of the X operation categories as well as in the primary X user environments. Individual tests include many types of Lines, Polygons, Text, Pixmaps, and Windows. **Suite X** addresses each functional area with the right combination of tests to produce meaningful results with minimal effort.

The results of Suite X show the tested system's ability to use available memory and graphics processors or accelerators. This information will help the user decide if their environment can benefit from additional hardware.

Subsystem Benchmark - Suite II

To evaluate a system's performance, the **Subsystem Benchmark - Suite II** tests the individual components of a UNIX computer system. The tests are conducted by repeating one of the 40 CPU instructions, system calls, or I/O transfers that **Suite II** exercises (the testing time is specified by the software, but can be customized by the user). The execution rate of each component is recorded, compiled, analyzed, and displayed in a report. **Suite II** measures the following seven basic hardware and software subsystems:

Disk	**Floating Point**
Function Calls	**IPC**
Math	**Memory**
System Calls	

AIM Performance Report Series and Subscription

The AIM Performance Report Series is a publication that contains over 100 of the most recent AIM Performance Reports on the newest UNIX computers from manufacturers such as AT&T, Bull, DEC, Data General, Encore, IBM, ICL, Motorola, NCR, Pyramid, Sequent, Solbourne, Sun, and Unisys. The series, published every other month, includes sections that describe the reports and the AIM products used to evaluate the systems.

A subscription service is available on an annual basis. The service includes the most current AIM Performance Series and all subsequent performance reports published by AIM during the next year (new reports are mailed bimonthly). For information about these products and services, call AIM Technology at (800) 848-8649 (outside CA) or (408) 748-8649.